ARCHITECTS ANONYMOUS

This *modellion* extended
overcomes problem of
triangular coffer

Chiesa dei Gesnati.   Venice.
12 July 1992
G. Massari archit. 1726

ARCHITECTS ANONYMOUS

QUINLAN TERRY

AD ACADEMY EDITIONS

Editorial Offices
42 Leinster Gardens London W2 3AN

COVER: Detail of the Pantheon, Rome. Photograph by Robert Stephenson
PAGE 2: Jesuits' Church, Venice
All illustrative material is courtesy of the author

First published in Great Britain in 1994 by
ACADEMY EDITIONS
An imprint of the Academy Group Ltd

ACADEMY GROUP LTD
42 Leinster Gardens London W2 3AN
ERNST & SOHN
Hohenzollerndamm 10713 Berlin
Members of the VCH Publishing Group

ISBN 1 85490 301 2

Distributed to the trade in the United States of America by
ST MARTIN'S PRESS
175 Fifth Avenue, New York, NY 10010

Printed in Italy

CONTENTS

PROLOGUE

Not long before Raymond Erith died he had a dream. He dreamt that he was at an architectural gathering and all his friends were there . . . Hugh Casson, Freddie Gibberd, the Good Shepherd, the Bad Shepherd, Basil Spence, and many more. And a great figure from the past – it might have been Vitruvius – came down to speak. He went up to Erith and said that, really, he was not much good, he should have done this or that; and he would have been so much better if he had spent more time measuring and drawing to scale. It was not a wholly depressing dream; in fact Erith woke up feeling elated. For while the Vitruvius figure had told Erith that his work was less than perfect, he had not spoken to the other architects at all.

Since then I have made a lifelong habit of drawing and measuring, and have filled over thirty sketchbooks with details taken, at home and abroad, of anything that looks good. It may be a whole facade if I can find a building with scaffolding; or it may be simply a baluster, or a staircase; it may be a door surround or a window, or a monument in a church. And if measurement is difficult, it is sometimes helpful to draw a group of buildings in perspective. It is in this way that one can begin to appreciate and understand why our forefathers did things the way they did.

The practice of drawing and sketching gives a proper perspective to the continuity of history. It demonstrates how the timeless principles of architecture have been applied at different times; and therefore how to apply them in our time. 'No new work of art comes into existence without an organic link to what was created earlier.' (Solzhenitsyn)

The sad truth today is that, speaking generally, architects (and art-historians) are unwilling to see history continuing through the present time, and that is why new buildings look out of place beside old ones. This attitude has led directly to the unpopularity of our profession, and in turn to the power of the conservation movement – who have the sympathy of the public whose experience is that what will go up will be inferior to what comes down. This means that when a twentieth-century Vanbrugh or Gibbs – or even a latter day Nash – is commissioned to work on any old building, he is restricted from designing in the old tradition on the grounds that this would falsify history. The historical continuity of classicism was approved throughout the seventeenth, eighteenth and nineteenth centuries but is forbidden in the twentieth. What is called 'genuine' in all the revivals up to the turn of this century is called 'pastiche' in this. Thus the continuity of architectural history is paralysed, ironically, by the nostrums of architectural historians; and the rise of architectural history as an academic degree subject runs parallel with the demise of classical architecture. Architecture has become something to be written about – not to be looked at, or built today – the written word counts for more than the visual image.

Nevertheless, the visual image is what the architect produces and by what he is judged. This image is made up of a great many factors – planning, construction, proportions, relation to its neighbours and finally and vitally – the detail. All these have been tackled through the ages and the results of this combination of art and expertise are all around us to see and to re-use.

To focus on an obscure or neglected building and to discover the hidden subtleties, the wisdom and ingenuity of its often nameless or forgotten author is the most valuable exercise for a practising architect. Inevitably, on closer study, accumulated knowledge and common sense come through and inspire one's own efforts at solving similar problems. Neither is this process new to our times: countless great buildings demonstrate their obvious provenance from uncelebrated antecedents. The great architecture of the Renaissance owes its entire existence to the study of anonymous architectural remains.

There is no record of the architects of the Pantheon or the Taj Mahal. Both grew out of the tradition around them: for one it was the simple unreinforced brick dome construction that had been practised in Rome for centuries; for the other it was Humayan's Tomb in Delhi. The workmen and the designers of great Gothic churches are nearly always unknown, bearing witness to the fact that tradition is of far greater importance in architecture than the name of the practitioner. It is essential to judge a building on its own merits – visual and structural, rather than to be fettered by a preconception governed by its historic importance and provenance.

All too often in these days of mass tourism and prolific art book production the eye is no longer used to focus on and to judge a work of art. The blinkered crowd stampeding for the Sistine Chapel, leaving the Raphael Loggias and all else in its wake is the extreme example of this malaise, but 'seeing with the ears' is not confined to the brainwashed amateur. We have largely lost the power to observe and to appreciate the unheralded beauty of the anonymous.

The great majority of the buildings shown on these pages are by unknown architects which demonstrates the importance of the tradition and the insignificance of the individual. It is hoped that this little book will help to burst some of the bubbles in this conceited age of architectural prima donnas.

Quinlan Terry

VII

THE DRAWINGS

Plate 1 – 26 Downshire Hill, Hampstead

I was born in this simple terrace house, built *c* 1820. It has a frontage of 17 feet and two rooms on each of its four floors. The front room is 13ft 2in x 13ft and the back room 10ft x 11ft 3in. The best room on the first floor takes up the whole frontage.

It is a typical example of the Georgian tradition for a larger terrace house adapted to the humbler circumstances of the artisan. The rooms are modest but adequate and even gracious in their simplicity. This is because the windows are well proportioned and well placed in the wall; the doors are panelled and have respectable plate architraves; the fireplaces have reeded surrounds; heights of rooms vary on each floor; there is a well made cut-string dog-leg staircase with a mahogany handrail and curtail. In fact there is everything that one needs for a civilized existence.

The terrace house formula – anonymous in its origin – has never been bettered for town living. There is no overlooking, no meaningless and dangerous space 'left over in planning' – everything fits together within an acceptable degree of asymmetry and great economy of design.

Plates 2 & 3 – 1 Alwyne Villas, Canonbury

There are endless possibilities within the terrace house discipline. This is a pretty, double-fronted example, built about 1810 with accommodation on three floors around a central staircase. The rooms are 14ft 6in x 11ft 10in. The front door is an ingenious design incorporating a version of the Doric order with a fluted pilaster and a fanlight which fits into the segmental portion of the circular arch identical to the circular headed sash windows on either side.

Plates 4-6 – The Mereworth Lodges, Kent

As an earnest but purely academic art-historian clutching his Pevsner approaches Mereworth Castle, he will probably drive past two lodges opposite the main gates. This pair of simple cottages has more of the rustic simplicity of the Veneto than all of Colen Campbell's efforts at the other end of the drive. They are timber-framed with a central brick wall to take the chimneys and a straightforward square plan which generates a three bay front elevation with central door and modillion[1] pediment. The ease and simplicity of the whole design is masterly; the front door case complete with plain six-panelled square-framed door, consoles and bold entablature appears both effortless and entirely appropriate.

Plate 7 – Trellis Porch at Copford, Essex

The carpenter on site was probably the author of this intricate trellis porch. Patterns range from the traditional criss-cross lattice over the entrance opening to the ingenious 'cobweb' and interlocking diamond shapes in the side panels. It is impossible to know whether these derive from some book of – perhaps Eastern – patterns, or are purely the result of the local tradition and other trellis porches copied by this carpenter.

Plates 8-11 – Shermans Hall, Dedham

A grander version of a double-fronted house built *c*1730 is an impressive and scholarly answer to making an imposing elevation in a street within a narrow frontage. On this little building, scarcely 25 feet wide, all the three orders are employed. A giant Doric in brick at the corners, a little Ionic in brick and stone around the central niche, and a Corinthian complete with pediment and modillions in timber around the front door.

Plates 12-15 – Well House and Old Grammar School, Dedham

These are typical good village houses of the early eighteenth century. Well House exhibits three versions of the Doric order: full height in brick for pilasters at the corners complete with triglyphs and guttae[2] in rubbed brickwork, a little order in the niche over the front door, and a larger order with a segmental pediment in timber around the front door itself.

The earliest windows (probably Queen Anne) have boxes on the face with a sloping bullnose cill, thick glazing-bars and deep splayed shutters in the reveals.

Plates 16 & 17 – The Custom's House, King's Lynn

This magnificent building commissioned in 1683 by Henry Bell, an antique dealer, employs all three orders: Doric on pedestal with imposts and arches for the ground floor; superimposed Ionic complete with modillions and pediment in the centre around the niche with the statue of Charles II; and Corinthian turret of cruciform plan, supporting an octagonal turret and weather vane, above the steep roof and a widow's walk.

Plates 18-22 – Higham Hall, Suffolk

The mediaeval part of this house remains near to the church, but the front was rebuilt in Suffolk White brickwork with overhanging Tuscan eaves and pediment in 1811, and shows the influence of Sir John Soane but in many ways improves on that architect's wilful detailing. The familiar pattern of five sash windows in arches has been ingeniously employed to conceal the irregular piers and modillions, only apparent after close measurement. It makes a virtue of an asymmetrical plan with good rooms of 15 feet span. The small study to the left of the front door is ideally arranged with a window placed asymmetrically to allow for the door swing. This thoughtful flexibility incorporated into the design exhibits a skill known to many country builders but often rejected by architects because of their doctrinaire views on symmetry.

The main internal doors are 3ft 1½in x 6ft 8¼in with panelled architraves and rosettes in the corners. The ovolo and bead moulding in the panels is characteristic of the period without being wilfully innovative and the same mouldings have been reduced with great skill for the shutters. The staircase is a textbook example of a cut-string with brackets and mahogany handrail with sweeps and curtail.

Plate 23 – The Staircase at Llanharen House, South Wales

This grand circular stone staircase has 6½in risers on segmental treads cantilevered out of the wall and resting on the tread below.

Plates 24 & 25 Dedham House

Another village house standing in its own grounds, this was built about 1830 but looks of earlier origin. It has sash windows of textbook quality; 3ft 11¼in between the reveals and 7ft 8in high with boxes set in the reveal and thin ($\frac{9}{16}$in) glazing bars. The shutters are in deep reveals with projecting shutter boxes. The Gothick fireplace came from another house and was installed in the dining room by Raymond Erith who greatly admired its masterly Gothick detail and enjoyed the stylistic departure from earlier work within the traditional chimneypiece construction.

Plates 26-30 – Combermere Abbey, Salop

The variety of nineteenth-century Strawberry Hill Gothick and the Gothic Revival is practised here by the unknown builders in their alterations to this Cistercian Abbey and great skill goes into the detailing. This can be seen in the main doors with Gothic cusps, pinnacles with cruciform panels, octofoil column shafts and lotus leaf capitals in the dining room and internal doors of Gothic design.

The cornice on the east front demonstrates the designer's familiarity with Palladian detail and also his skill at crossing this with Gothic by adding trefoil modillions.

Plate 31 – Rowlands, Ilminster

This is a familiar and highly practical sixteenth-century detail of a leaded light window with label and gable in domestic architecture, before the advent of the sash. There is no better way of throwing rainwater away from the window opening and protecting the jambs from the weather.

Plates 32-39 – Dedham Church

The mediaeval detail of 1492 is employed with great skill and understanding both at the entrance porch and even more ingeniously at the arches and piers of the nave arcade. Here the designer alternates piers with capitals and piers without capitals where the mouldings of the arch run right down to the pier bases. The master mason who worked out the geometry of this scheme was obviously aware of all the subtleties of form in three dimensions and showed his ability with great competence.

The tracery to the West window demonstrates another facet of a great and continuous tradition which was applied for several centuries.

The main pinnacle, measured when the tower was being repaired, is an interesting piece of sculpture designed to be seen from 100 feet below. Few would realise that the octagonal buttresses have been surmounted by a hexagonal stone constructed in five tiers of poppyheads culminating with a weather vane.

Undoubtedly one of the glories of English mediaeval churches is their classical re-ordering after the Reformation. It is the best illustration of the continuity in architecture where Gothic and Classic mix together, each enhancing the other. The memorial to William Burkitt in the Chancel, erected in 1703, is a fine example of Baroque detail and shows how the English masons were not a wit behind their Italian counterparts. The plainness of the main cornice and little pediment, the form of the top and side urns, the symmetrical lamps, the fruit and flowers, festoons, drapery, lettering, gadroons [3], consoles and the acanthus leaf bases – all in veined white marble – form a masterpiece of design and carving. No name can be put to this little essay in Baroque memorial sculpture.

Plates 40-48 – St Helen's Church, Bishopsgate
After the Reformation the most interesting and inspired re-ordering took place at St Helen's which resulted in the injection of some very fine examples of Baroque stonework and joinery into this ancient mediaeval structure.

The Gothic tradition, well represented in the piers and arches and the tracery, thus became a backcloth to the great variety of sixteenth-, seventeenth- and eighteenth-century monuments for which the church is renowned.

The south door's Portland stone surround constructed in 1633 with its rusticated Doric pilasters, pulvinated frieze and broken pediment, has a wonderfully jubilant and lighthearted air – a real showpiece in the sombre mediaeval wall. Inside this stone surround a pair of oak doors is a virtuoso piece of joinery – with false perspective in the door panels, a centre meeting rail elaborately fluted and a semi-circular head with scrolls and a richly carved centrepiece.

The Pickering Monument, which was erected in 1574 by an unknown designer, employs the Corinthian order to Palladian proportions and detail, but combines it with the strapwork detail of the Netherlands, Bramantesque coffered arches and an ingenious arrangement of pilasters at the ends, where the Corinthian capitals are matched by a fleur-de-lys – a game not untypical of Michelangelo. There are gadroons, gnulling [4] and scrolls on the sarcophagus and an elaborate circular cartouche rises from the middle of the canopy.

The west doorcase with a Corinthian order on pedestal, swan-neck pediment with swags and a smaller segmental pediment above is even grander than the south doorcase. The door panels are again in false perspective.

The hexagonal Jacobean pulpit is another lively Baroque piece made up of panels containing a free adaptation of the order and a broken pediment with false perspective in the elliptical centres.

Plate 49 – St Mary the Virgin, Oxford

Not many designs in this country can surpass the audacity of the South door to St Mary the Virgin in Oxford. Here a most flamboyant piece of Baroque design is recklessly juxtaposed, without compunction, onto a typical large Gothic church. The architect obviously had enormous fun using all the tricks of the trade – the Corinthian order on Solomonica columns, several breaks in the entablature, volutes at the side, a broken segmental pediment with reclining figures and a niche breaking through the centre. For good measure, and so as not to be outdone by the Gothic work behind, he has made the keystone with fan vaulting.

Plates 50-51 – Il Duomo, Syracuse

On a much larger scale and even more outrageous, this splendid facade of the Duomo in Syracuse is the eighteenth-century contribution to the fifth-century BC Greek Temple of Athena. The original Doric colonnade still forms the side elevation and the greater part of the nave, but the new Baroque front, ignoring all precedent, employs a giant Corinthian order. No room here for the simplistic attitude of our planning and conservation bodies where mixing of orders is deemed a prime offence when adding to old buildings. The masterly composition of coupled Corinthian columns and pilasters with a central segmental broken pediment, every possible break in the elaborate entablature, the sculpture and the enrichment are in complete contrast with the rustic simplicity of the Greek Doric behind it. The result is a magnificent building admired by everybody; but it is only by measuring and drawing that the finer points of such complicated geometry can be fully appreciated and understood.

Plates 52 & 53 – St Niklas Church and a Doorway in Celetna, Prague

There should always be a continuous traffic in two directions in taking from one another's knowledge and expertise. The great and famous often draw their inspiration from the wisdom of local tradition and the rank and file reinterpret the achievements of the high fliers. Often a whole town or district bears the stamp of a famous architect who spent his working life there – but closer examination reveals that the architect's work is derived from the anonymous local tradition which he studied and made his own.

I noticed this very clearly in Prague where the work of the Dientzenhofer family not only dominates the skyline, but has penetrated the general street scene, made up of that exquisite Baroque detail for which Prague is justly famous. The door to St Niklas Church was designed by the celebrated Kilian Ignaz Dientzenhofer in 1732-35. The doorway to a patrician house in Celetna Street is just one of many anonymous examples of the Baroque tradition which became a natural way of building in that city.

Plates 54-56 – The Queen's College Chapel, Oxford

This chapel, built in the early 1700s, is probably the combined work of Dean Aldrich – a man of taste who had more than a passing knowledge of Palladio's *Quattro Libri* – and a good local builder, John Townsend. The result is a highly orthodox and inspired use of the classical orders with all their enrichments exquisitely executed in stone and stucco. The coved ceiling with its ribs containing shell and acanthus motifs and the hexagonal coffering over the East end indicates that the designer was aware of Palladio's measurements of Nimes. The ironwork to the Communion Rail with its scrolls and leaves is of outstanding quality and detail.

Plate 57 – The King's Staircase, Kensington Palace, London

This piece of wrought iron is worthy of the great master of this trade – Tijou. This very useful and adaptable pattern has inspired many similar balustrades since. The construction of the staircase itself is made up of stone treads $12\frac{3}{4}$in x 6in high, cantilevered from the wall in the traditional manner.

Plates 58 & 59 – Organ Case at Warminster, Wiltshire

There is a name on this beautiful organ case built in 1792. G P England not only made the organ but also designed the casing. In those days it was assumed that the man who controlled the tone of the pipes and the arrangement of the keys was also the most competent to arrange the visual appearance of the pipes within the case. The flat fields have additional non-speaking pipes – in order to make the design look right. The carved work of the shades, the acanthus leaf bracket, shells and urns all make this a very fine and competent piece of late eighteenth-century architecture.

Plates 60-63 – Chinese Temple at Amesbury Abbey, Wiltshire

This little temple, which was erected in 1780, is connected with the name of Sir William Chambers and shows a clever adaptation of Palladian mouldings in a light-hearted Chinese direction. Much of the joinery looks more like the design of the carpenter on site than the architect.

Plates 64-67 – Castletown Cox, County Kilkenny

This grand house was built in 1767 to the design of Davis Ducart, a Sardinian who practised in Ireland in the mid-eighteenth century. It has all the features of English Palladianism but has been carried out by a designer familiar with the Baroque work of Italy; this is particularly obvious in the design of the architrave mouldings. A practical knowledge of carpentry construction has been combined with competent use of architectural mouldings in the turret design. The carpenter's contribution takes the major part here but the ornamentation would have been the architect's responsibility.

Plates 68-73 & 76– Fatehpur Sikri, Agra

This fascinating group of buildings commissioned by the Emperor Akbar (begun in 1570 and abandoned 14 years later), is an eclectic mixture of Hindu and Mogul details in stone, clearly derived from wood construction. Such was the strength of the local pink sandstone and the scarcity of timber that strutts, tie beams, stairs, grilles and even roof tiles were made of this stone. In spite of the wide range of stylistic sources, this is a remarkably consistent piece of architecture. Its consistency is dictated by the practical requirements achievable by the material used to govern the size and proportions of its architecture. It is classical in all but name, because it is composed of columns, pilasters with capitals and bases, dosserets,[5] architraves, cornices with large overhanging shades, arches, blocking courses, balustrades, domes and pinnacles.

There is no record of any named architect; if there was one, he would certainly have been a master mason.

Plates 74-75 – Red Fort, Agra

Once again, there is no named architect. And here again the underlying principles of classicism endure as can be seen in the detail of the base and capital, the capital having squinches[6] in place of the echinus[7] so to fill the interspace from a twelve-sided shaft to a square abacus. The ogee arch with cusps is the Eastern counterpart to the cusped Gothic arches of the West.

Plate 77 – Humayan's Tomb, Delhi

This great building, designed with almost Bramantesque consistency, is again by an unknown designer. It is earlier than the Taj Mahal in Agra and is generally regarded as its inspiration.

Plates 78 & 79 – Brick Kiln at Bulmer, Tye, Sudbury

Some years ago I made a study of unreinforced domes in Rome and the Middle East. The brick kiln at Bulmer was, however, the first entry in the sketchbook which was devoted to this subject. It fits well here because the anonymity of its construction is indisputable and its architectural status is of the humblest degree.

XIV

Nevertheless, the principle of its construction – albeit on a small scale – demonstrates how the intelligent and practical use of materials leads to a perfect solution of a difficult problem.

Nor is this a new thing, since the spanning of a circular opening in brick was practised by the Romans 2,000 years ago. The 'stickiness' of lime mortar, the need to eliminate wooden centring and the inert quality of lime concrete masonry (which did not expand or contract with changes in temperature) were uppermost in the minds of these men. The builders of the Pantheon were familiar with this technique and used it with such skill and vision that they achieved the greatest span in the world, which has not been surpassed since.

Plate 80 – Cornice of the Pantheon, Rome

I felt compelled to measure the cornice of the Pantheon although – or perhaps because – so many great architects have done it before. This, the greatest of anonymous buildings, has been an inspiration and an example to countless generations; the great dome and portico have a remarkable effect on everyone who sees it.

But it is only by measuring and drawing a piece of architecture that one can assimilate all the complexities of the design. There is no other way, no short cut to acquiring this accumulated common sense and knowledge which is tradition. The result well repays diligent study.

Finally, it should be said, that this method of study pays little regard to all the modern materials and methods of construction with which we are provided by the age in which we live. Indeed, such method will have little application today, whilst the modern approach demands such respect and maintains the overwhelming power it has retained for the last seventy years. Doctrinaire modernism and post-modern classicism have one quality in common: to avoid every building material and method of construction which has hitherto worked. It was a personal conceit of Raymond Erith, and of mine also, that such old materials and proven methods are in fact better; and that we shall again come to believe the wisdom of old, as we see the collapse of the new.

February 1994.

Notes
1 A small block or bracket of which a series is frequently used as the support of a cornice.
2 Small drop-like projections under the triglyphs of a Doric architrave.
3 Decorative patterns formed of a series of convex ridges.
4 Convex and concave flute in three-dimensional form, particularly vases and sarcophagi, which gives greater effect to the shape.
5 The French term for an additional block or slab set on top of a capital; sometimes called a super-abacus.
6 Arches built over the angles of a square structure usually to support a spire or dome.
7 The convex moulding or ovolo of a capital supporting the abacus.

Plates

26 Downshire Hill, London N.W.3.

June 1968

Sixteenth scale

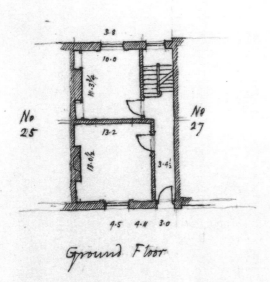

Ground Floor

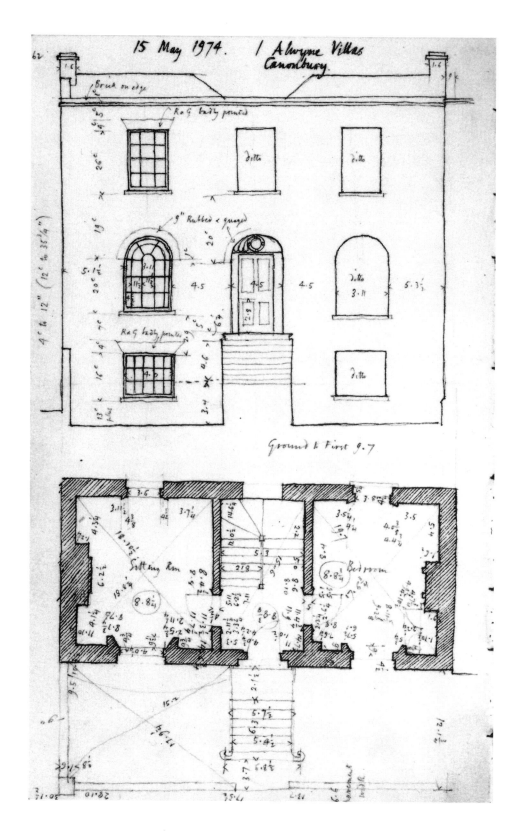

15 May 1974.   1 Alwyne Villas
Canonbury.

Ground & First 9.7

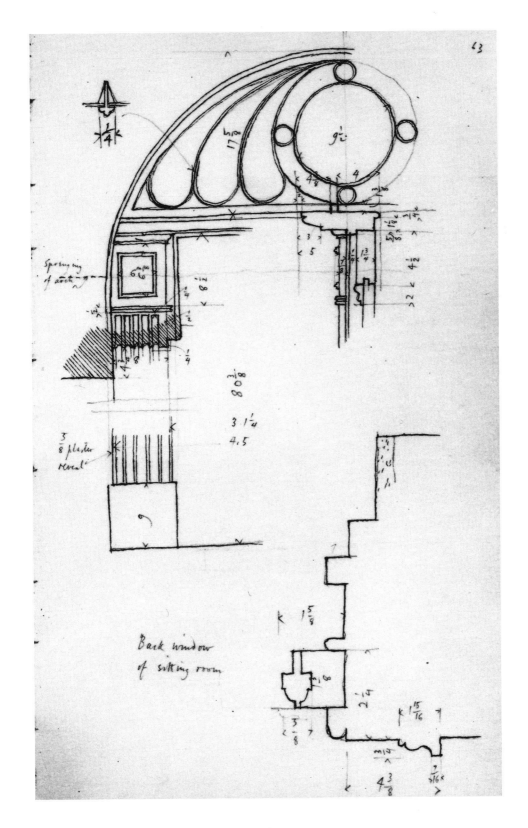

Spring of arch

Back window
of sitting room

3/8 plaster
reveal

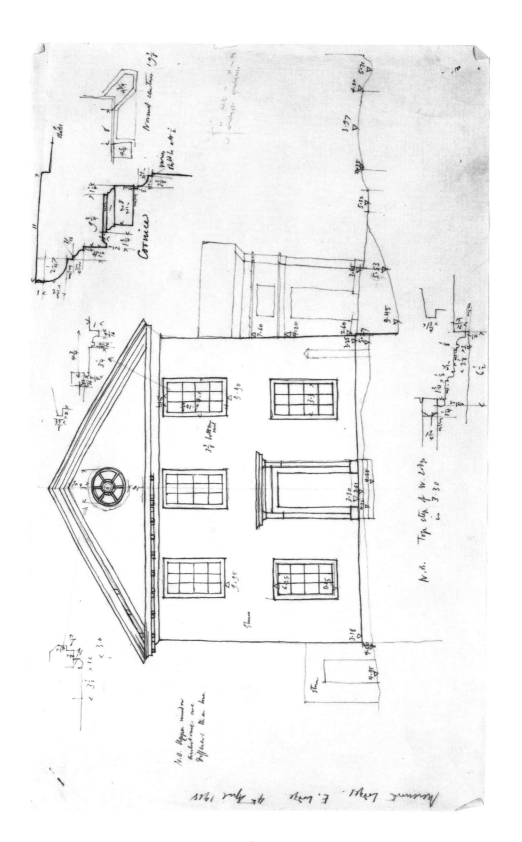

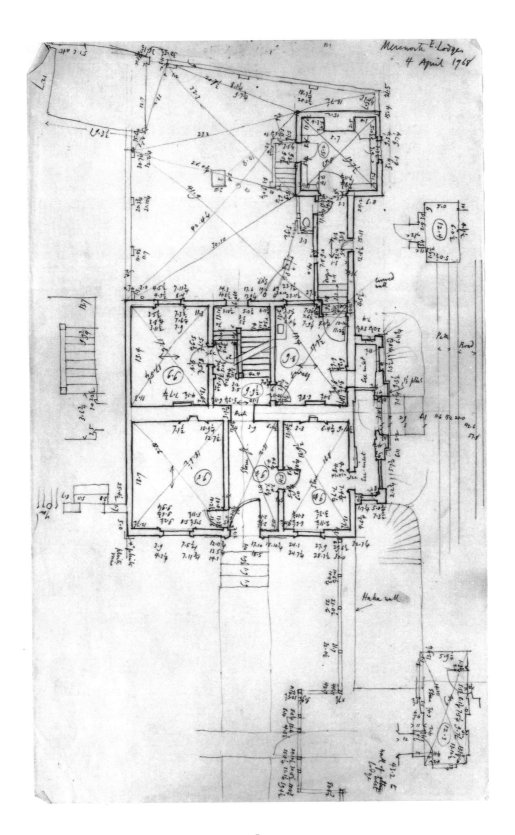

Merewortu E. Lodge
4 April 1968

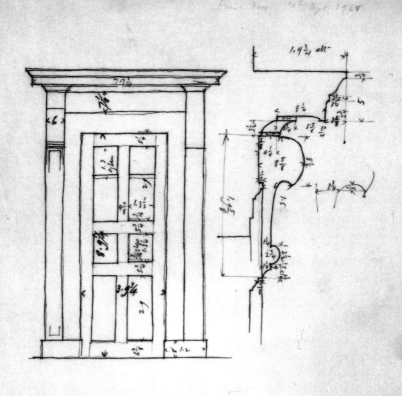

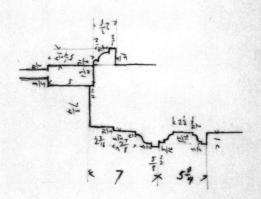

Mereworth E. Lodge. Front door
10 Apl '68

6

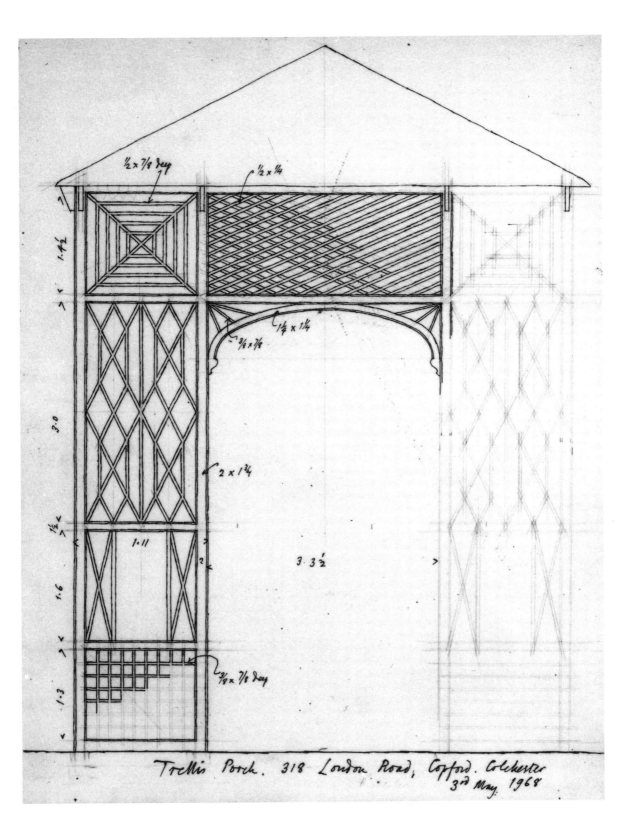

½ x ⅞ deep

½ x ¼

1¼ x 1¼

¾ x ⅞

1.4½

3.0

2 x 1¾

1.11

1½

1.6

3.3½

3/8 x ⅞ deep

1.3

Trellis Porch. 318 London Road, Copford. Colchester
3rd May 1968

7

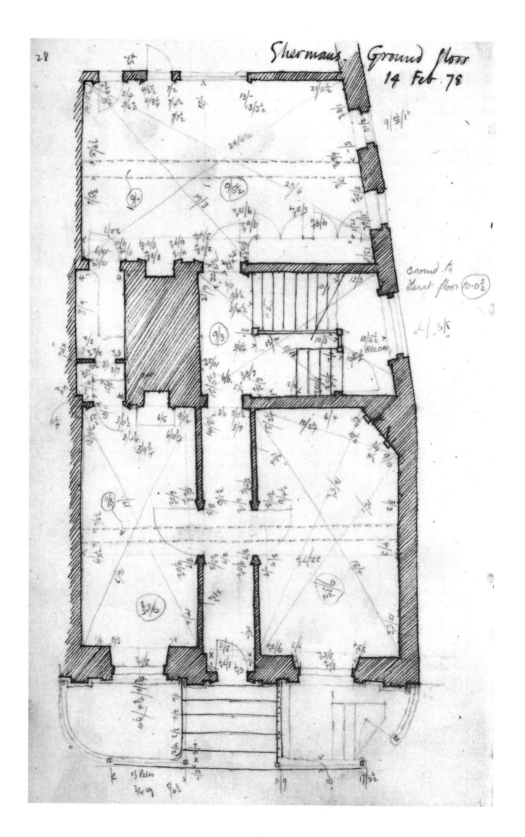

Shermans, Ground floor
14 Feb 78

Sherman's Hall, Dedham
9 Nov '77

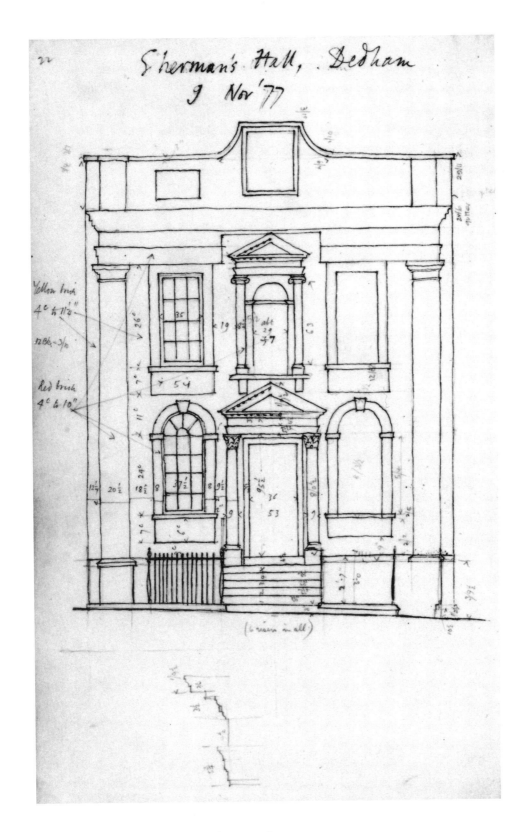

Yellow brick
4" to 11½"

12 Bk = 3/0

Red brick
4" to 10"

(6 risers in all)

9

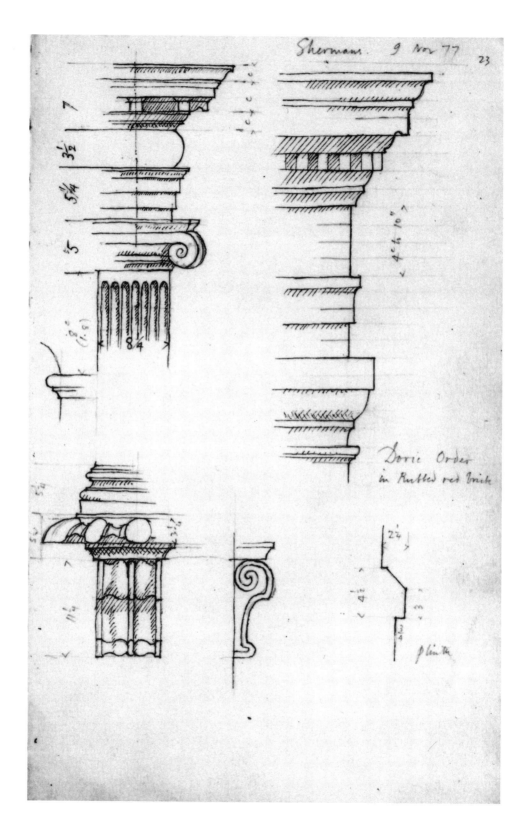

Doric Order
in Rubbed red brick

plinth

Shermans.   9 Nov '77

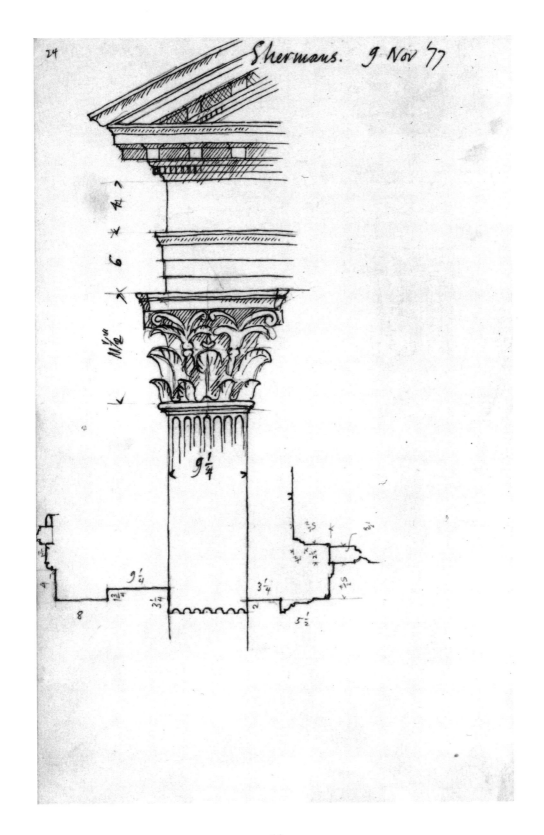

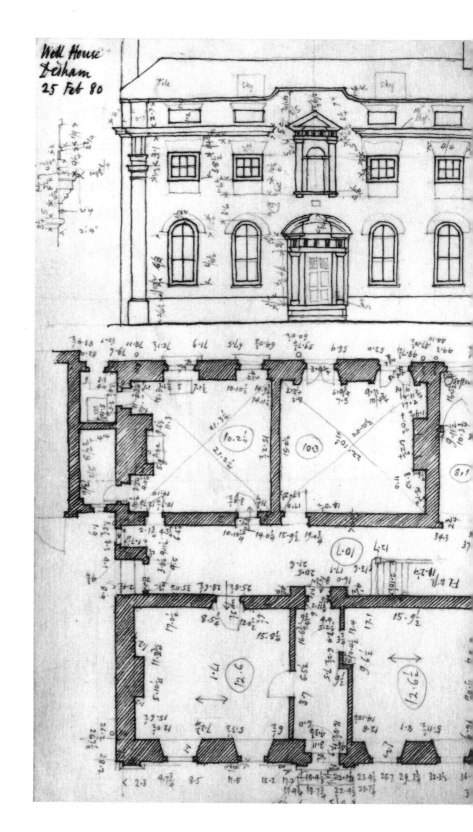

Well House
Dedham
25 Feb 80

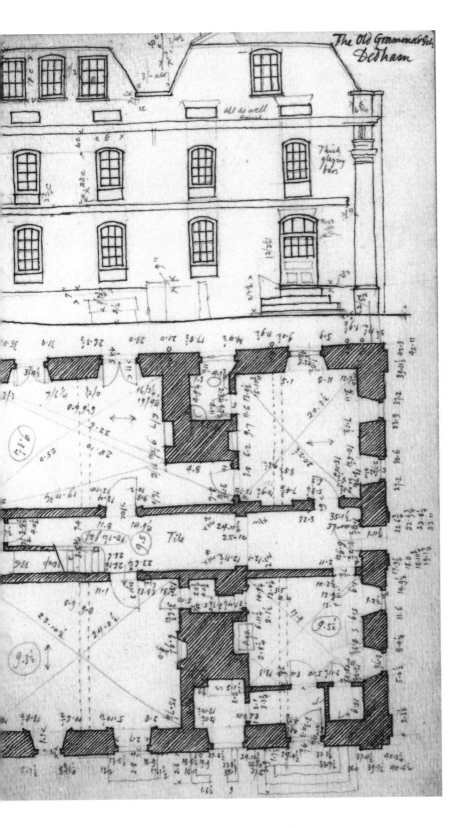

The Old Grammar Sch.
Dedham

all as well course

Thick glazing bars

Tile

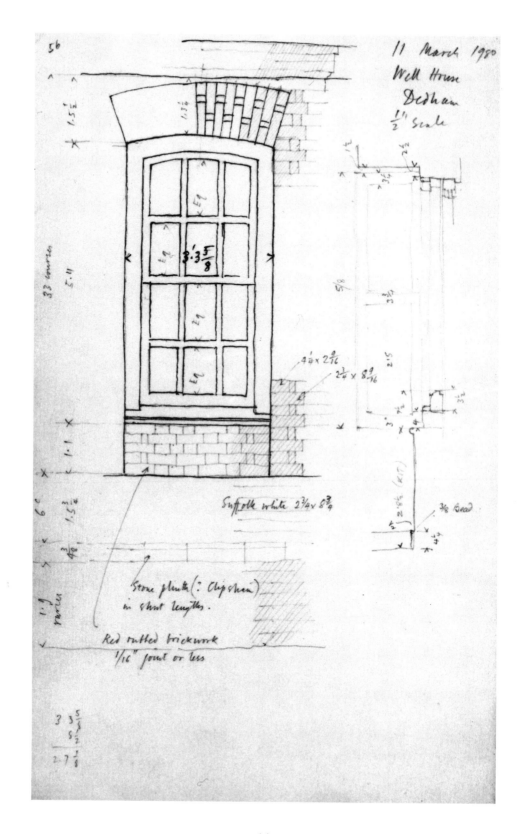

56

11 March 1980
Well House
Dedham
$\frac{1}{2}''$ Scale

33 courses

$1.5\frac{1}{2}$

$1.3\frac{3}{4}$

5.4

E.q

E.q

$3.3\frac{5}{8}$

E.q

E.q

1.1

6 c

$1.5\frac{3}{4}$

$\frac{3}{4}$

1:9
rebate

Suffolk white $2\frac{3}{4} \times 8\frac{3}{4}$

$4\frac{1}{4} \times 2\frac{9}{16}$

$2\frac{3}{4} \times 8\frac{9}{16}$

Stone plinth (: Clipsham)
in short lengths.

Red rubbed brickwork
$1/16''$ joint or less

$5/8$

$3\frac{1}{2}$

2.5

$3''$

$2.9\frac{1}{2}$ (KT)

$\frac{3}{8}$ Bead

$3 \; 3\frac{5}{8}$
$\frac{5\frac{1}{2}}{2.7\frac{1}{8}}$

14

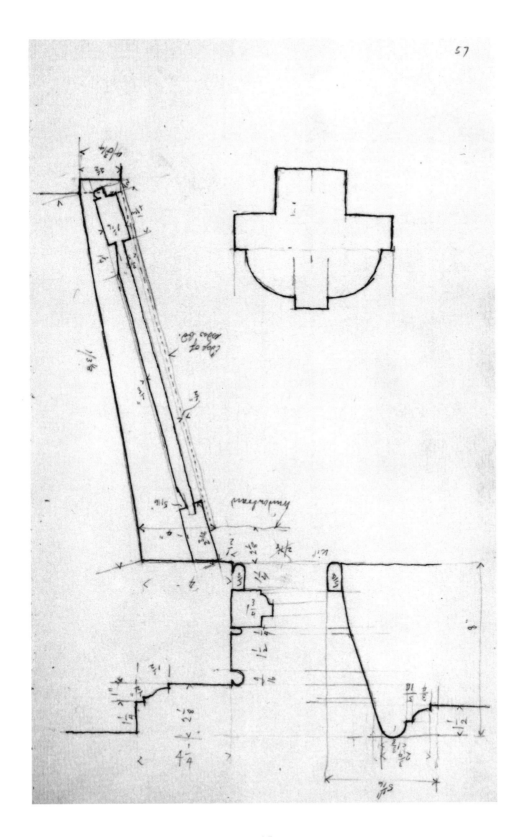

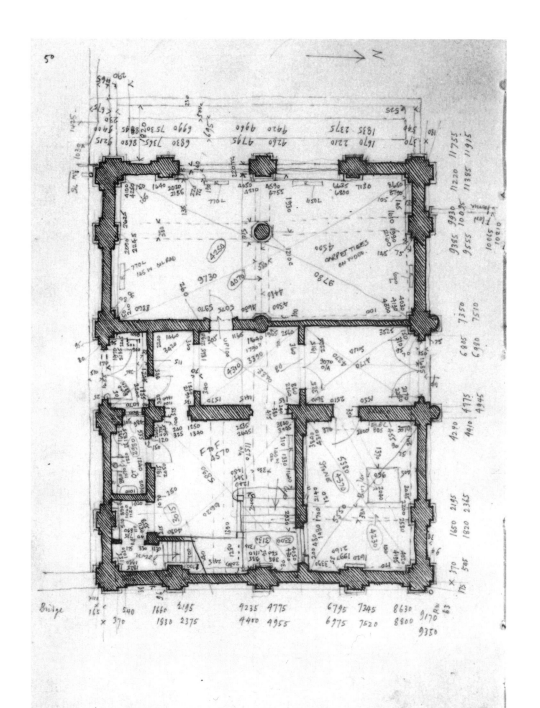

The Custom's House. Kings Lynn
26 Sept '90

16

The Custom's House
King's Lynn
13th Sept '90

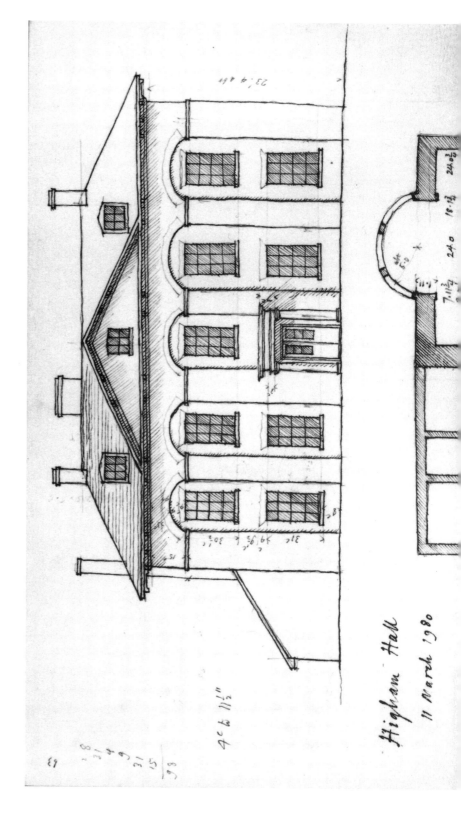

Higham Hall

11 March 1980

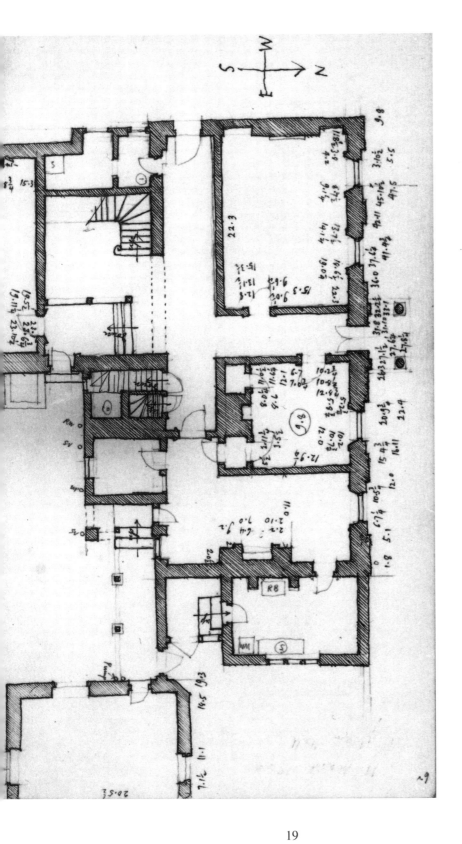

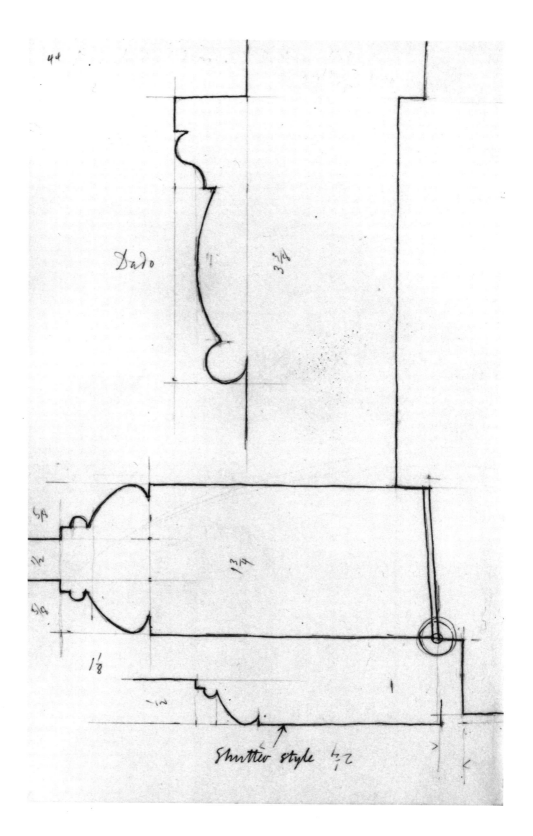

Dado

3/4

1 3/4

1 1/8

Shutter style 2 1/4

Main internal door   Higham Hall   27 Apl 1990

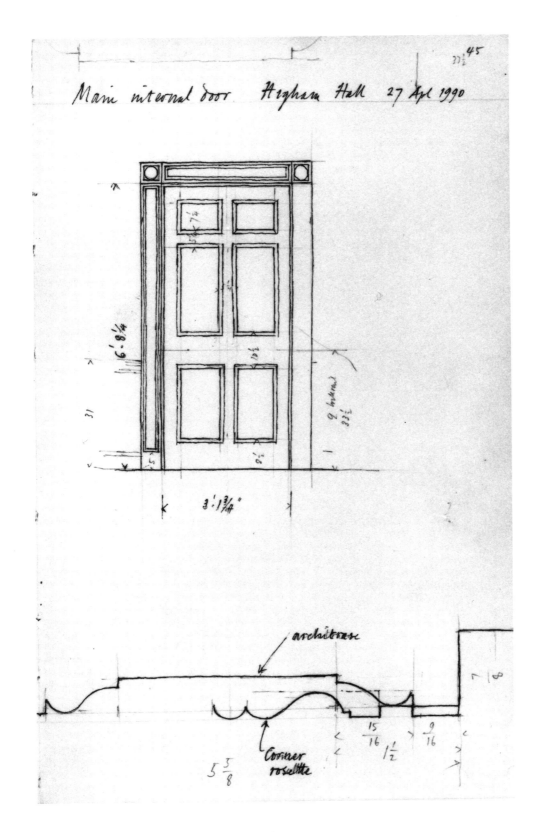

architrave

Corner
rosette

5 3/8   15/16   1 1/2   9/16

3' 1 3/4"

6' 8 1/4

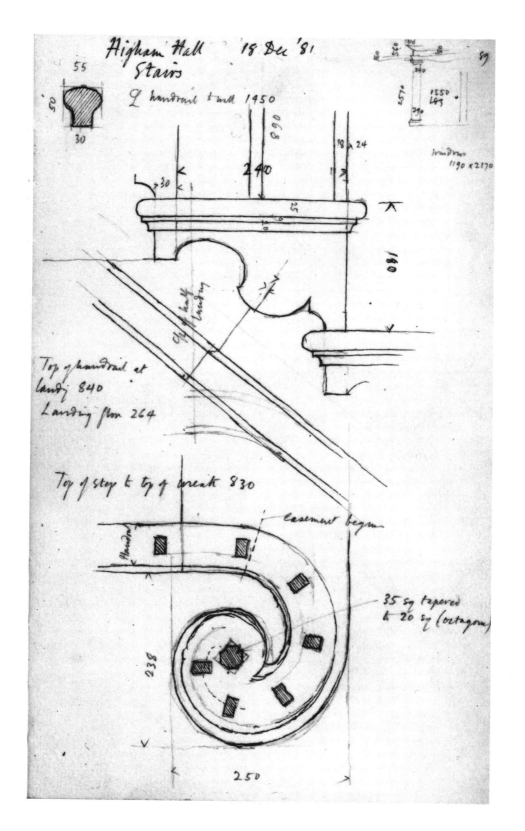

Higham Hall   18 Dec '81
Stairs

55

50
30

⌷ handrail + well 1450

890

240

18 h 24

30

25

180

Top of handrail at
landing 840
Landing flow 264

Top of step to top of wreath 830

easement begun

Handrail

238

35 sq tapered
to 20 sq (octagon)

250

windows
1190 x 2170

1550

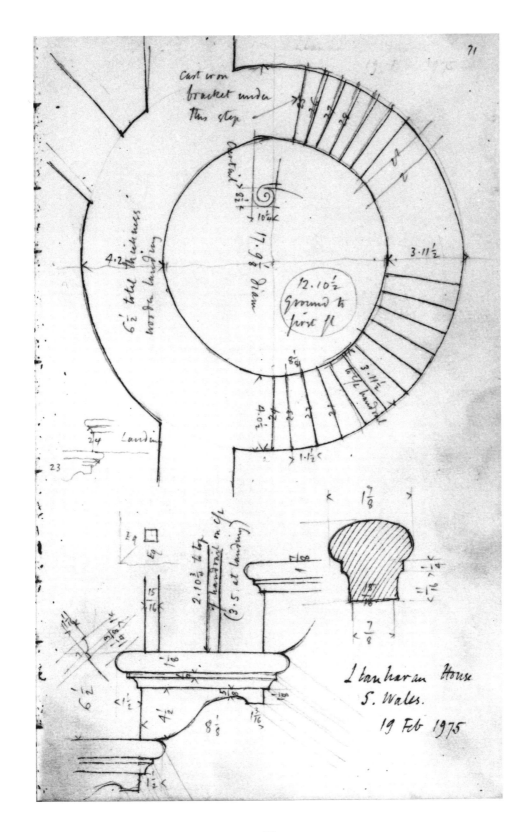

Cast iron
bracket under
this step

Central

6½' total thickness
both to landing

4.2

10½ ck

17.9½ Diam

12.10½
Ground to
first fl

3.11½

8'

4.0½

3.11½
to ½ handrail

1.1½

Landin

24

23

2.10¾ to top
½ handrail in c/l
(3.5. at landing)

15/16

1/16

1/16

6'½

1½

4'½

8⅛

1 9/8

7/8

18/16

7/8

5/16

13/16

Llanharan House
S. Wales.
19 Feb 1975

23

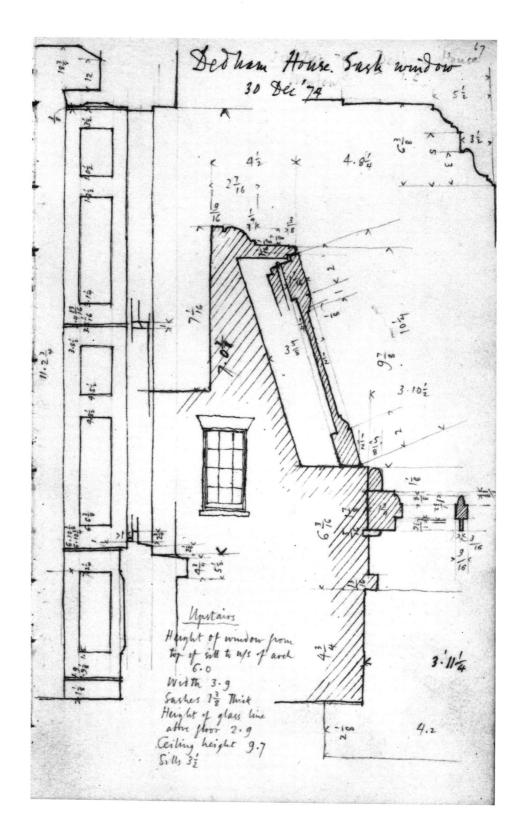

Dedham House. Sash window
30 Dec '74

Upstairs
Height of window from
top of sill to u/s of arch
6.0
Width 3.9
Sashes 1⅜ thick
Height of glass line
above floor 2.9
Ceiling height 9.7
Sills 3½

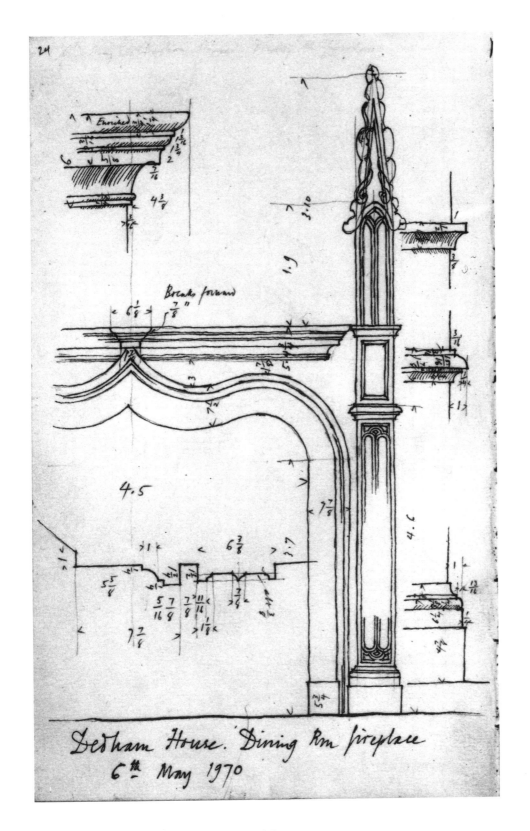

Dedham House. Dining Rm fireplace
6ᵗʰ May 1970

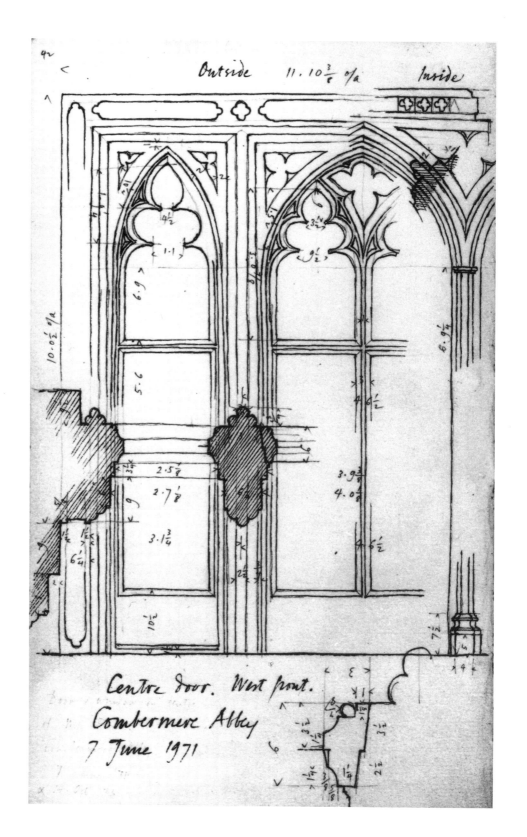

Outside   11.10$\frac{3}{8}$ o/a   Inside

Centre door. West front.

Combermere Abbey

7 June 1971

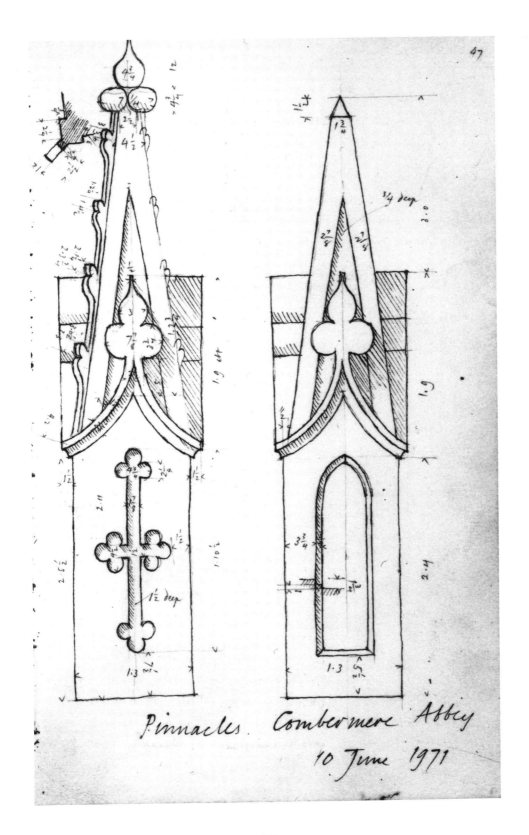

Pinnacles. Combermere Abbey
10 June 1971

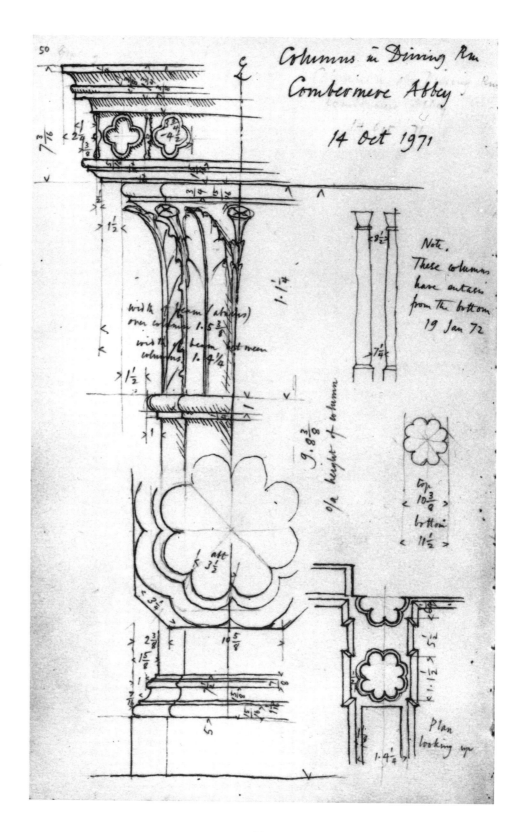

Columns in Dining Rm
Combermere Abbey.

14 Oct 1971

Note.
These columns
have entasis
from the bottom
19 Jan 72

width of beam (abacus)
over column 1.5 3/8
width of beam between
columns 1. 4 1/4

9.8 3/8
o/a height of column

top
10 3/8
bottom
11 1/2

Plan
looking up

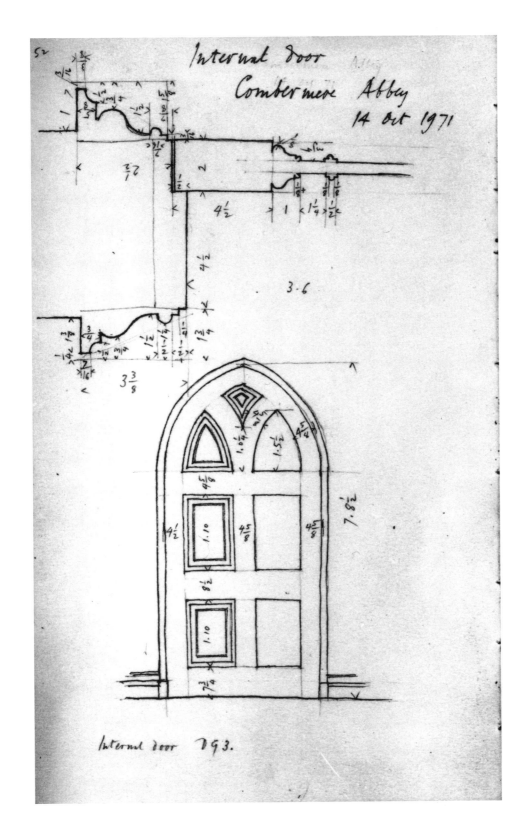

Internal door
Combermere Abbey
14 Oct 1971

3·6

Internal door ℔ 3.

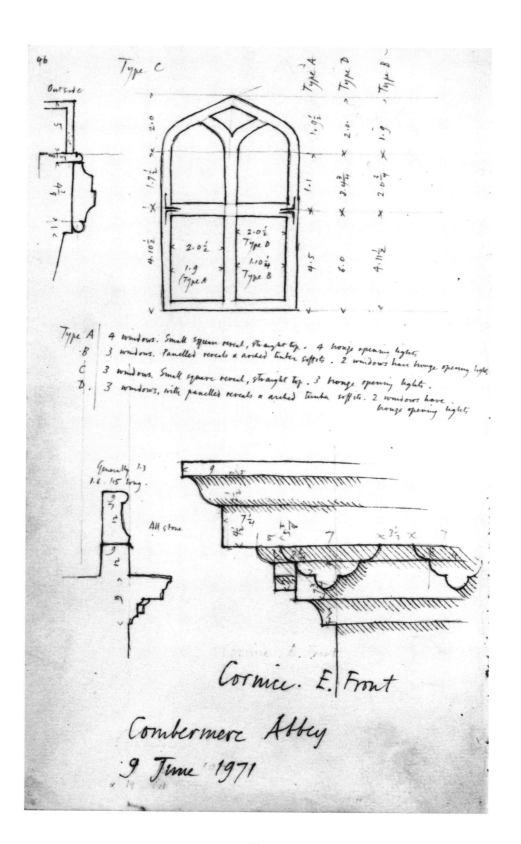

Type C

Outside

Type A
Type D
Type B

2.0½
Type D

1.9
(Type A

1.10¾
Type B

Type A | 4 windows. Small square reveal, straight top. 4 bronze opening lights.
.B | 3 windows. Panelled reveals & arched timber soffits. 2 windows have bronze opening lights.
C | 3 windows. Small square reveal, straight top. 3 bronze opening lights.
D. | 3 windows, with panelled reveals & arched timber soffits. 2 windows have
                                                        bronze opening lights.

Generally 1.3
1.6. 1.5 long.

All stone

Cornice. E. Front

Combermere Abbey

9 June 1971

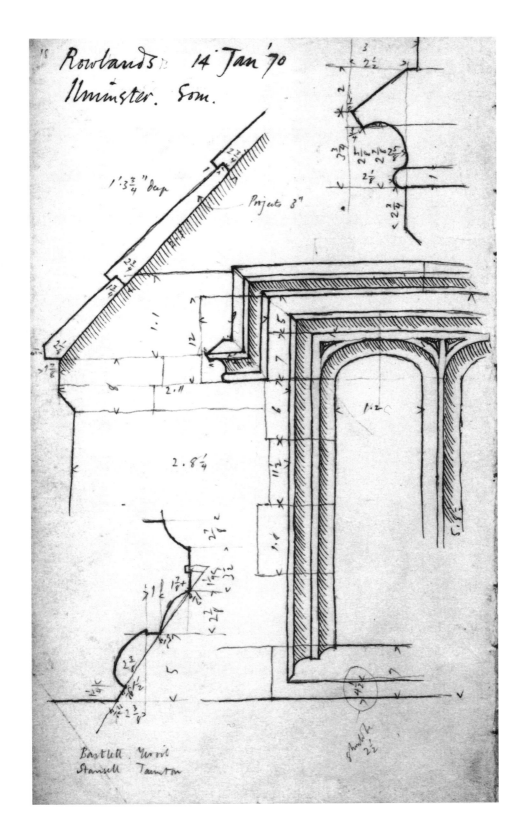

Rowlands 14 Jan '70
Ilminster. Som.

1'·3¾" deep

Projects 3"

Bartlett. Wood
Stansell Taunton

31

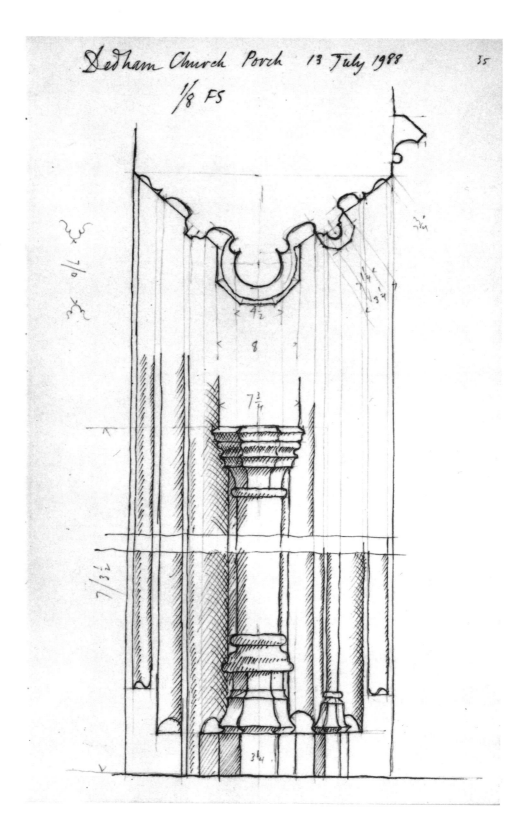

Dedham Church Porch   13 July 1988

1/8 FS

32

Dedham Church.   Pinnacle   21ᵃ Apl 92

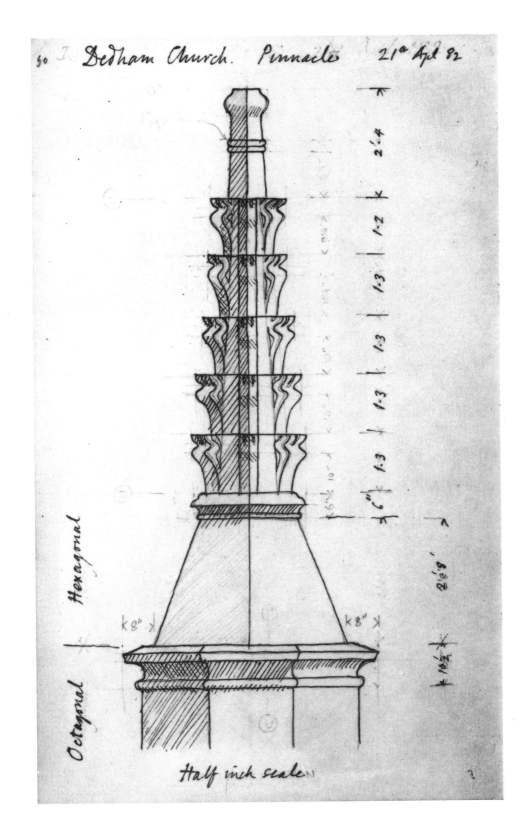

Hexagonal

Octagonal

8"

8"

2·4

1·2

1·3

1·3

1·3

1·3

6"

2'·8"

10½"

Half inch scale

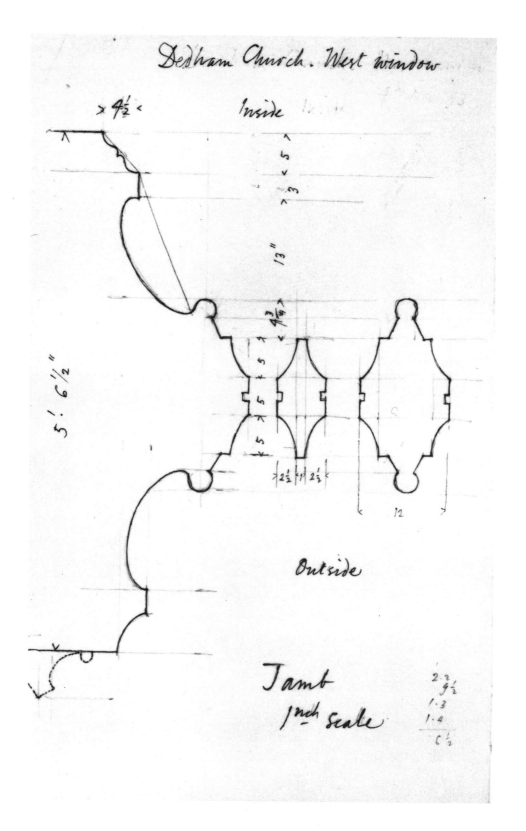

Dedham Church. West window

Inside

× 4½ ×

13"

4¾

5' 6½"

2½ | 1 | 2½

12

Outside

Jamb

inch scale

2.3
9½
1.3
1.4
6½

34

2.4   6   2.4   1½/12

Dedham Church. West Window

½" Scale. 4th Nov 93

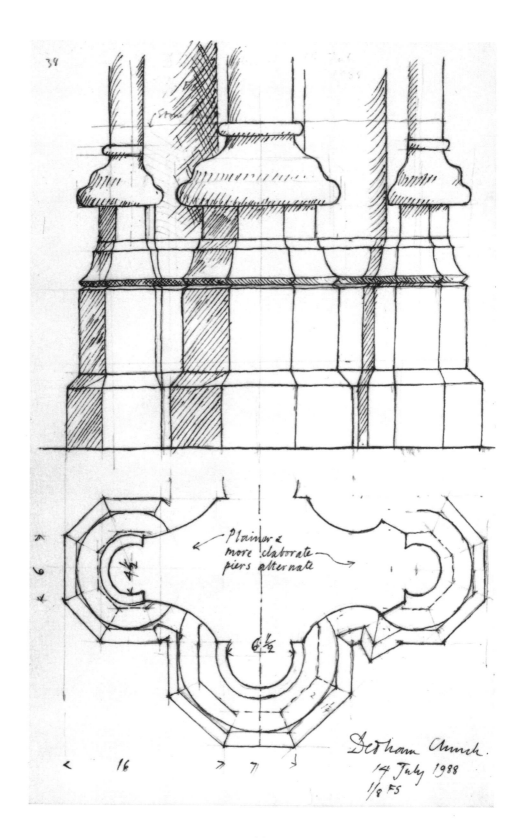

38

Plainer &
more elaborate
piers alternate

6½

16   7   7

Dedham Church.
14 July 1988
1/8 FS

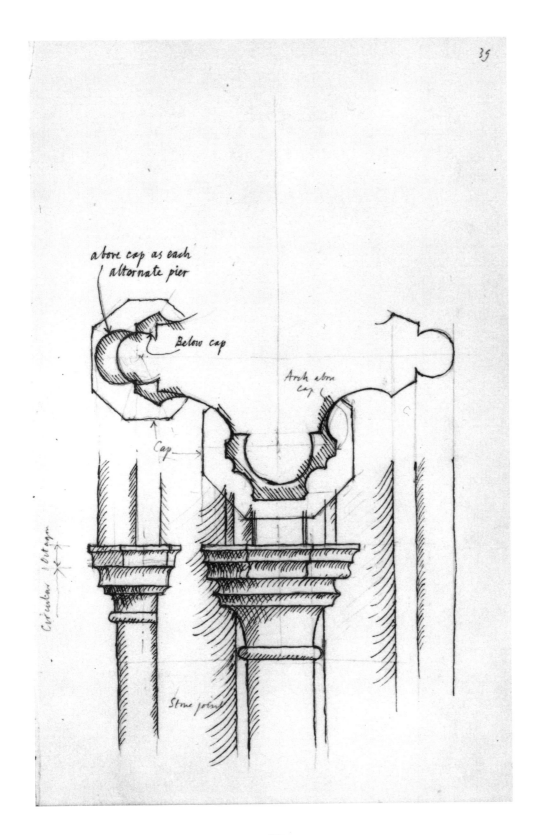

above cap as each
alternate pier

Below cap

Arch above
cap

Cap

Circular & Octagon

Stone joint

37

6 Burkitts Memorial, Dedham Church   14 June 1976

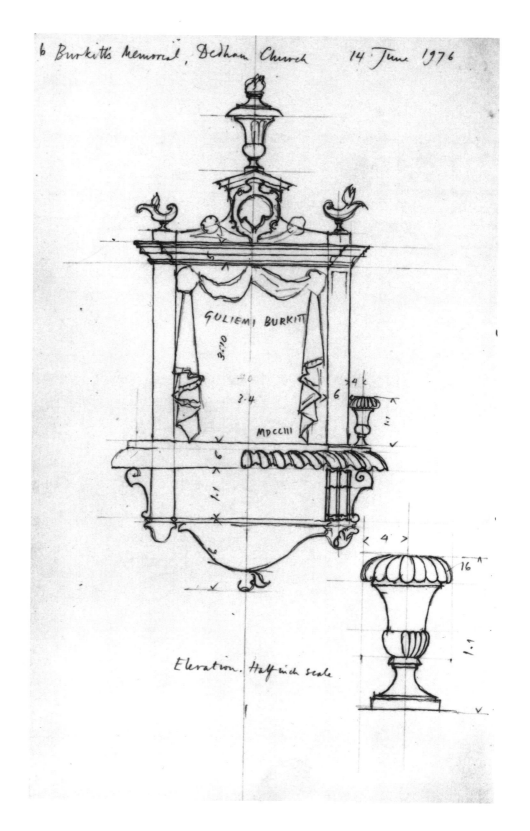

GULIEMI BURKITT

MDCCIII

Elevation. Half inch scale

38

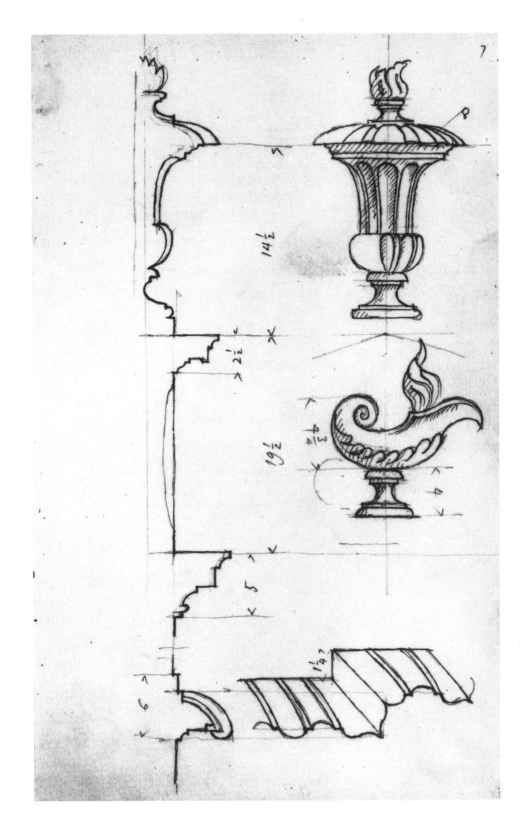

South Door Surround. Half inch scale

S. Helen's Bishopsgate

24 July '92

40

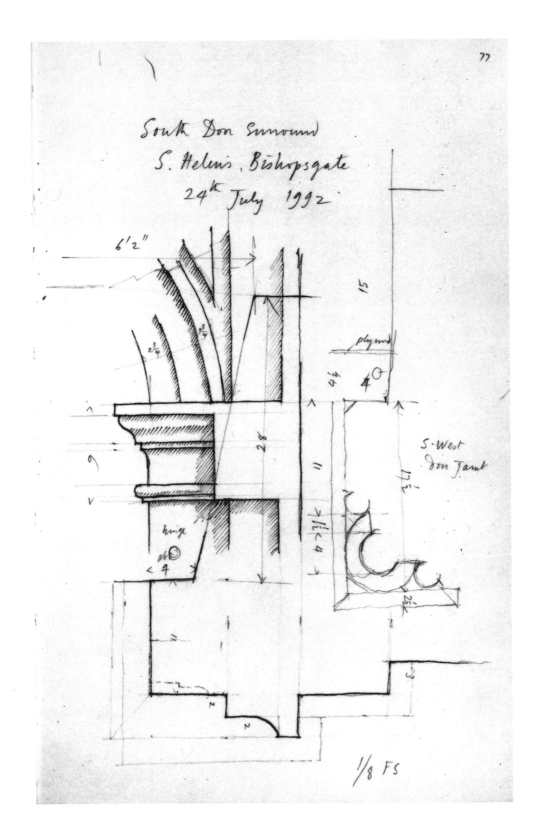

South Door Surround
S. Helens, Bishopsgate
24th July 1992

6'2"

2¾

¾

28

15

plynd

4

4

S·West
Door Jamb

17½

hinge

4

4

25½

1/8 FS

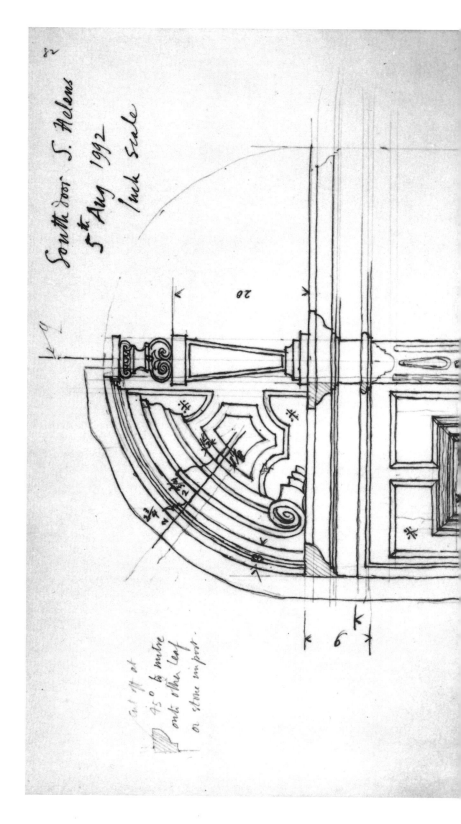

South door S. Helens
5th Aug 1992
Inch scale

cut it at
45° to mitre
onto other leaf
or stone impost.

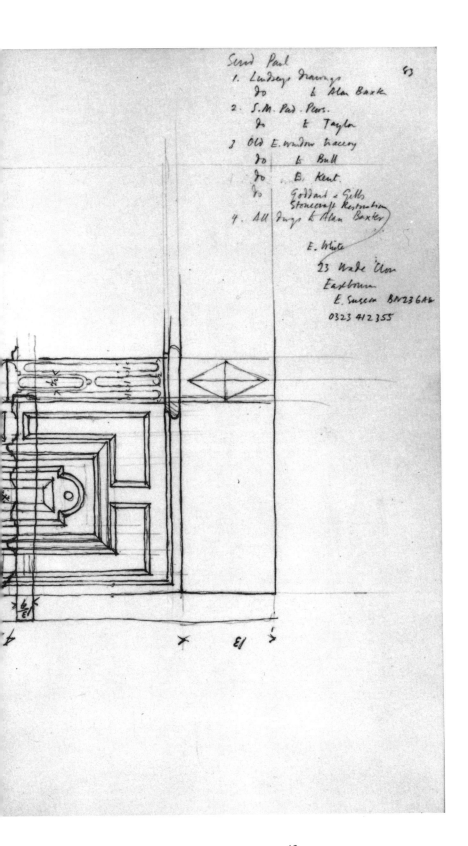

Send Paul
1. Lindseys drawings
        do   to Alan Baxter
2. S.M. Pad. Pews.
        do   to Taylor
3 Old E. window tracery
        do   to Bull
        do   ...B. Kent.
        do   Goddard & Gibbs
                  Stonecraft Restoration
4. All dwgs to Alan Baxter

            E. White

        23 Wade Close
        Eastbourne
            E. Sussex BN23 6AZ
        0323 412355

43

3rd Feb 1993
Pickering Monument
S. Helen's Bishopsgate
1/2" Scale & 1/8 FS

pillow

pillow

Side elev. of pilasters

Sarcofagus on
plinth

45

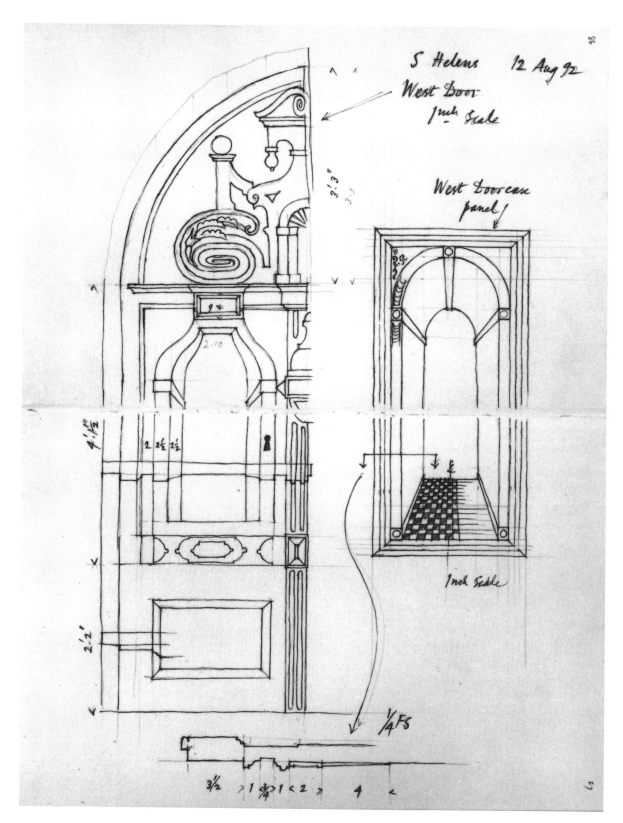

S Helens   12 Aug 92

West Door
Inch Scale

West Doorcase
panel

3.3"

Inch Scale

¼ FS

46

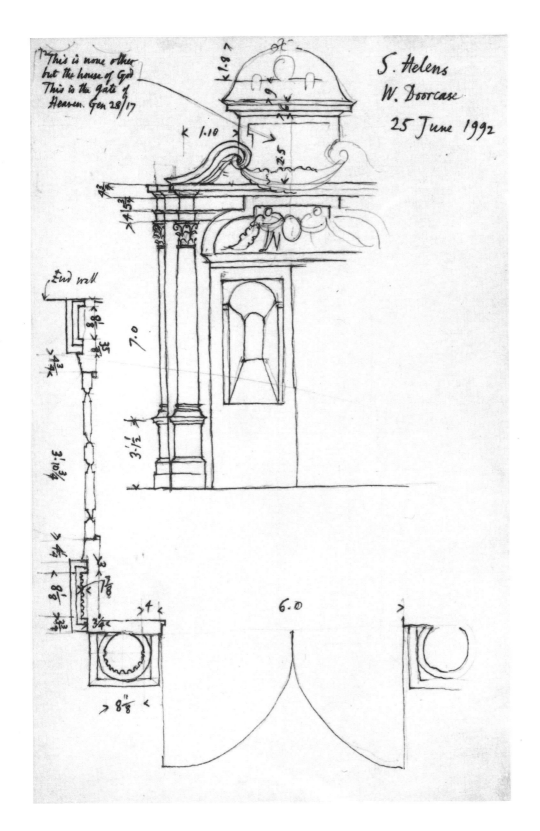

This is none other but the house of God This is the gate of Heaven. Gen 28/17

S. Helens
W. Doorcase
25 June 1992

End wall

47

Panel on pulpit. S. Helens   30 Oct '92

¼ F.S. Scale

k   12"   ᴣ

5   0.1   6   4.0

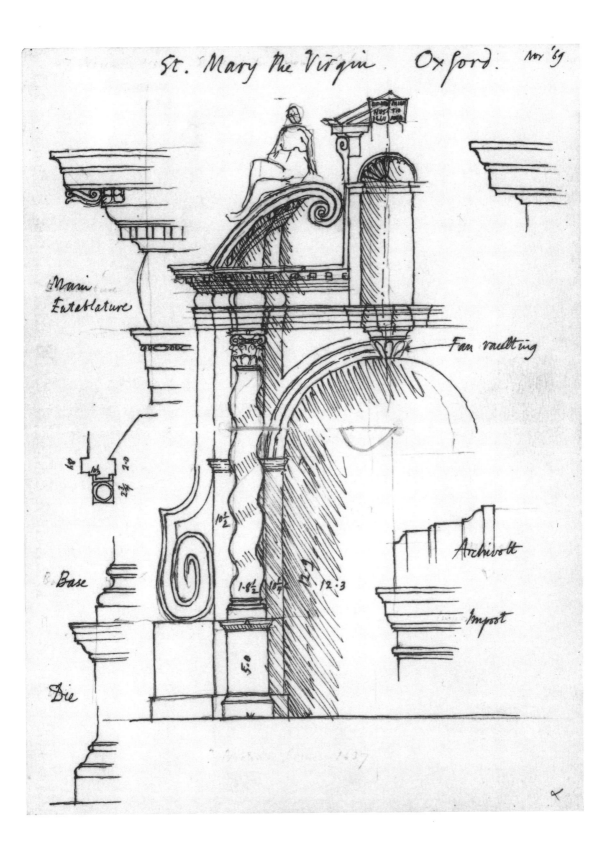

St. Mary the Virgin.   Oxford.   nov '69

Main
Entablature

Fan vaulting

Archivolt

Impost

Base

Die

10½

1·8½   10⅞   12·7   12·3

5·0

49

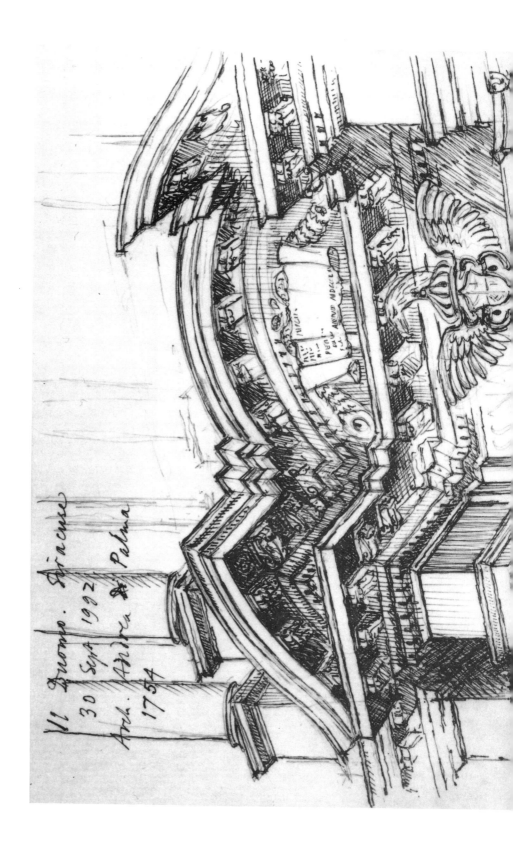

Il Duomo. Siracusa
30 Sept 1992
Arch. Andrea di Palma
1754

50

51

Doorway in Celetna. Prague
29 Sep 89

53

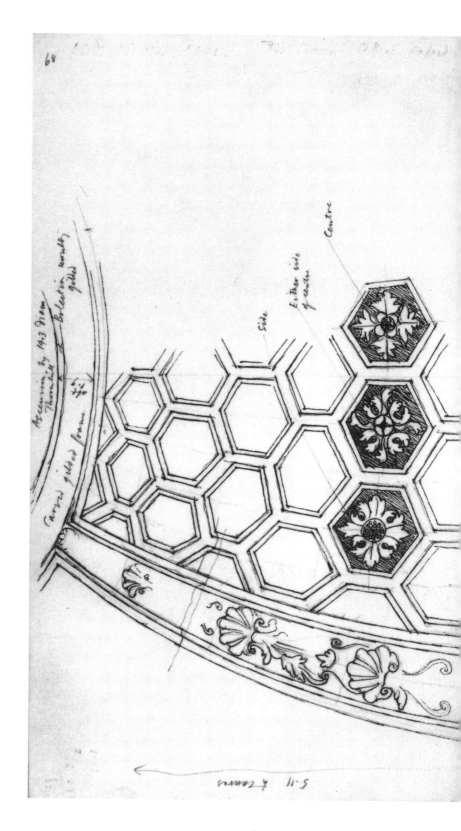

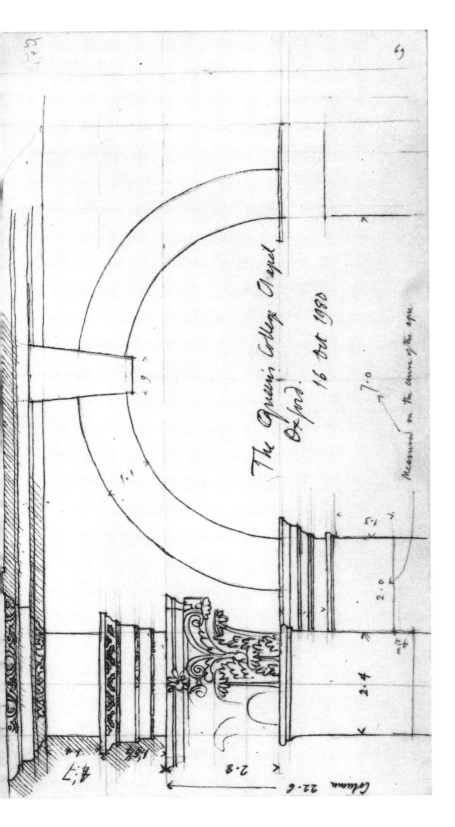

The Queen's College Chapel
Oxford.
16 Oct 1980

Measured on the axis of the apse

Column 22·6

The Queen's College, Chapel
Oxford 16 October 1980
Communion rail in wrought iron
1/8 F.S.

3/8 × 3/4

3/8 round

5

6

7/8 round
No 2

Leaf beaten out
of 1/16 flat by 1/4

No 3

3/16 × 8 clips

7/8 × 7/8

24

3·2¼

3/8 × 3/4

7½

16

No 20

3

No 4

This pattern inserted in the
middle to make up the
uneven number of twists.

1½

3¼

6

Handrail to wall
8'·4"

12¾

The Kings Staircase
Kensington Palace.
14 Feb. 1978

2⅞

1⅞

7/8

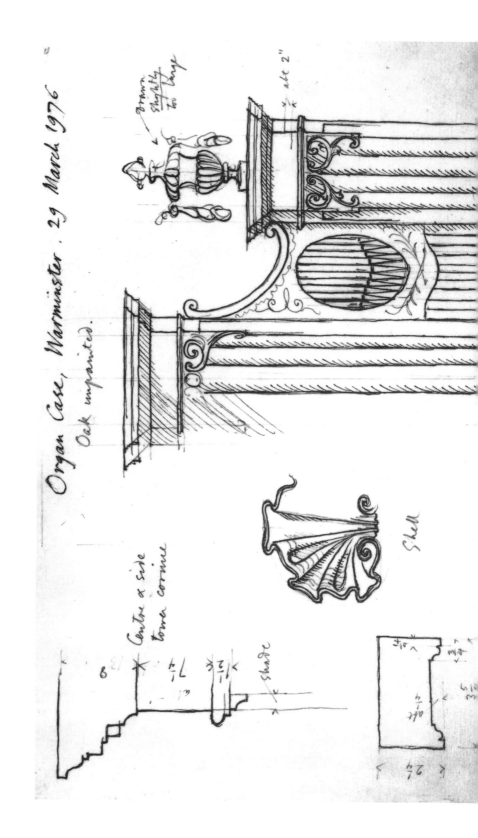

Organ Case, Warminster . 29 March 1976

Oak unpainted.

Centre & side
tower cornice

Shell

Londini Fecit 1792

ENGLAND

N.B. Pipes in Side
towers project
slightly. This is
accompanied by projection
in shade at top.

Side tower

Impost

C. Bracket.

7.6

5

59

Chinese Temple
Amesbury Abbey
28 July 1975

N ←

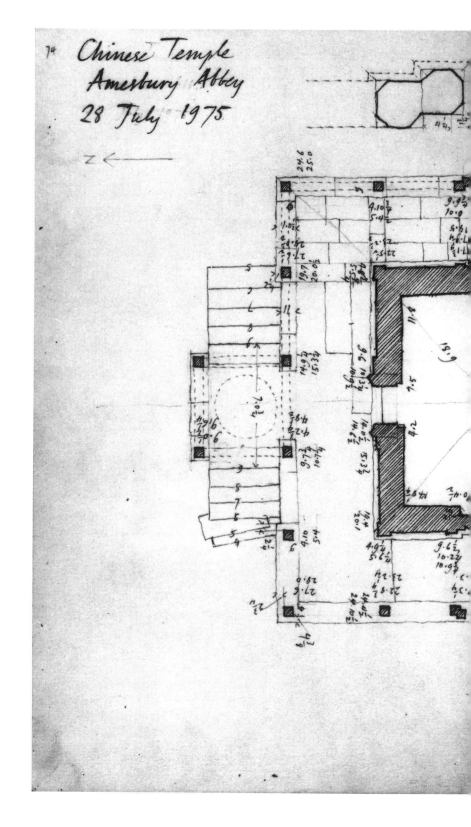

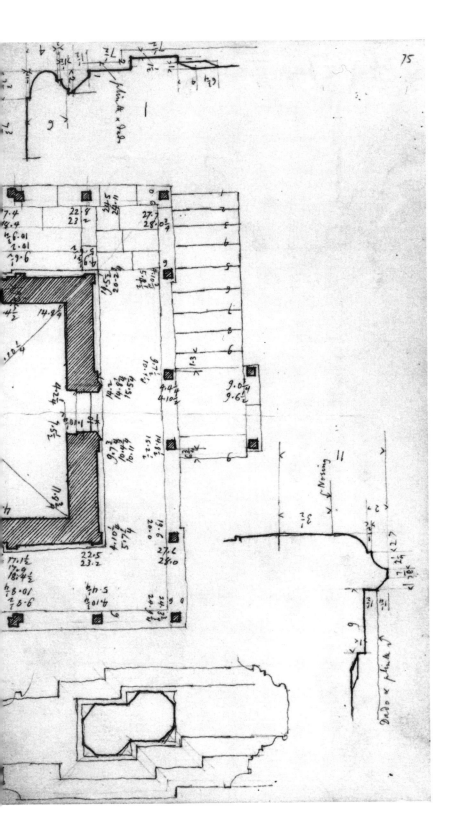

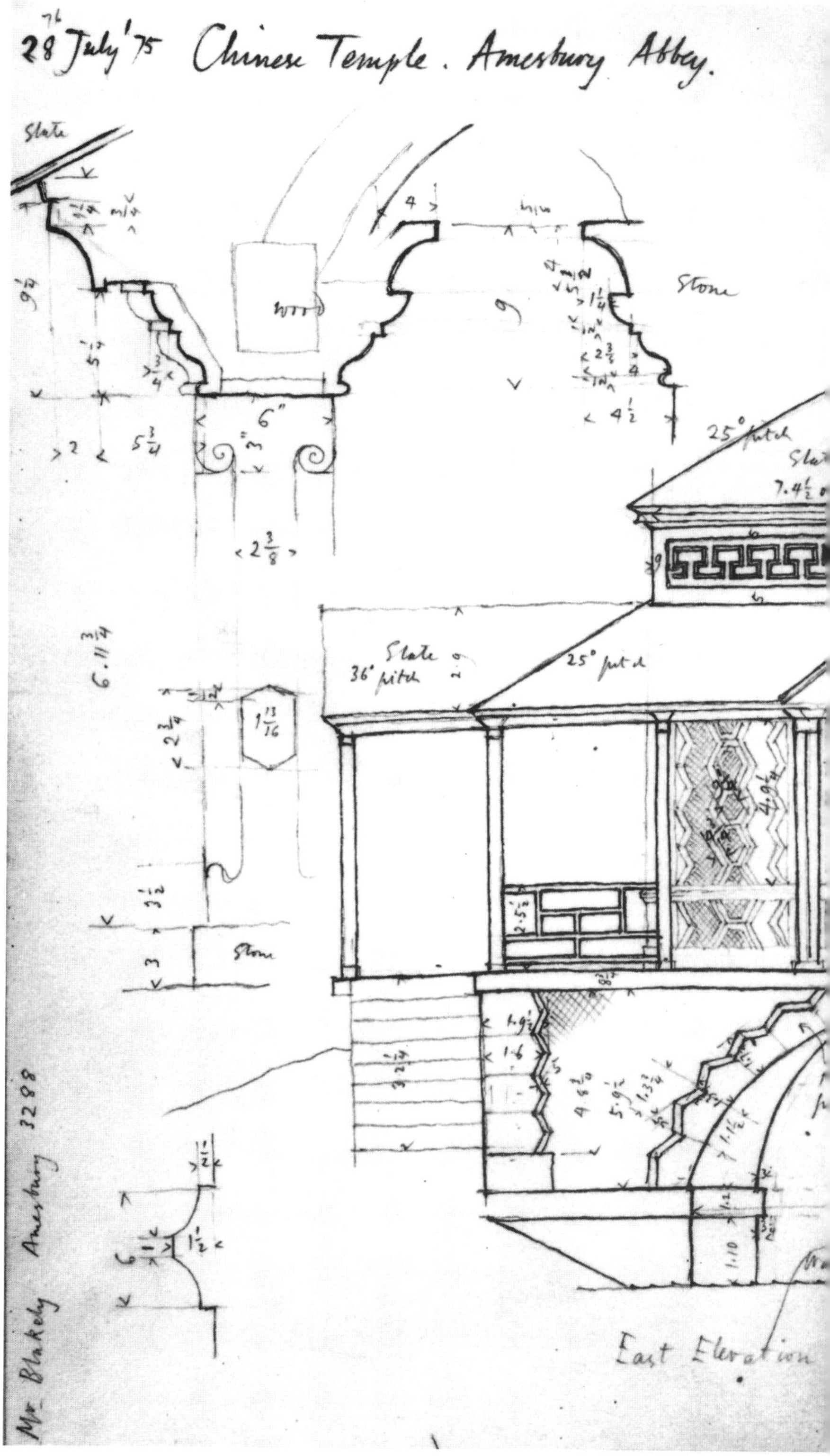

28th July '75 Chinese Temple. Amesbury Abbey.

Slate

Stone

25° pitch
Slate
7.4½

Slate
36° pitch

25° pitch

Stone

Mr Blakeby Amesbury 3298

East Elevation

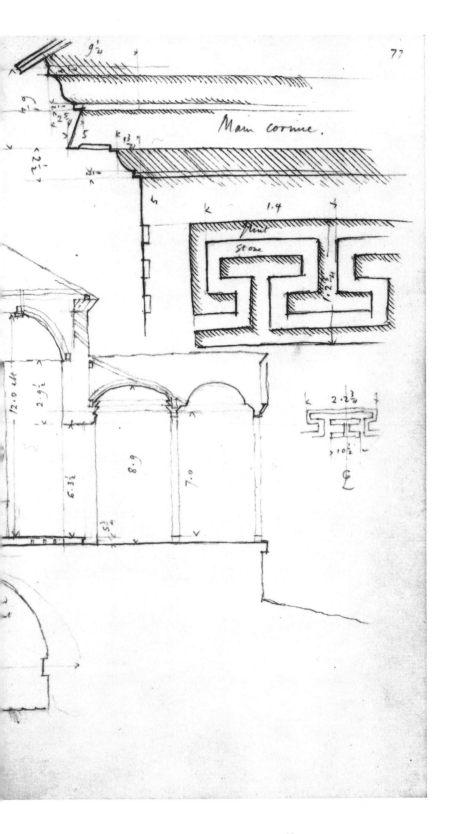

Main cornice.

flint
stone

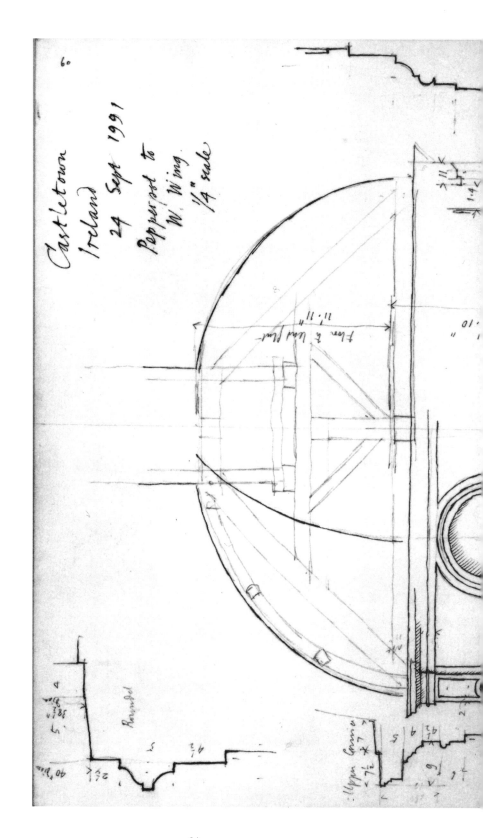

Castletown
Ireland
24 Sept 1991
Peppered to
W. Wing.
1/4" scale

60

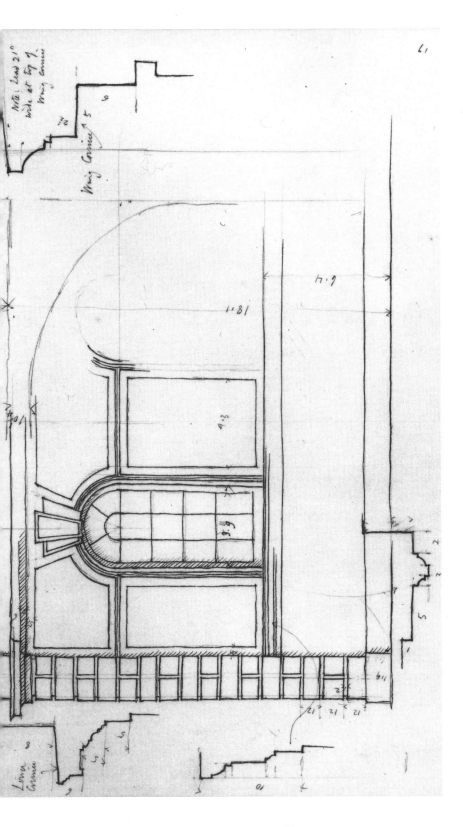

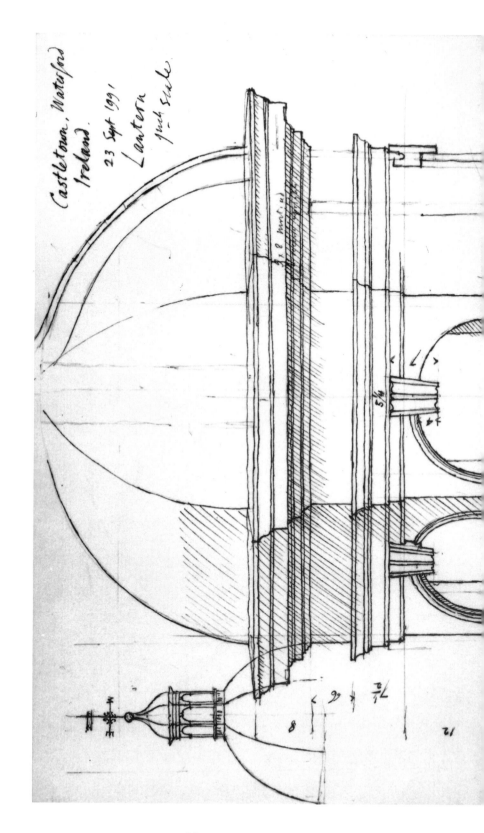

Castletown, Waterford
Ireland.
23 Sept 1991.
Lantern
full scale.

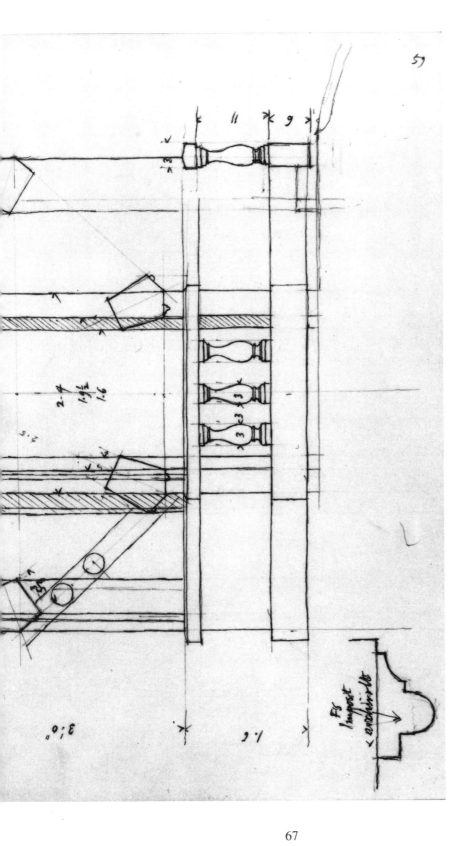

67

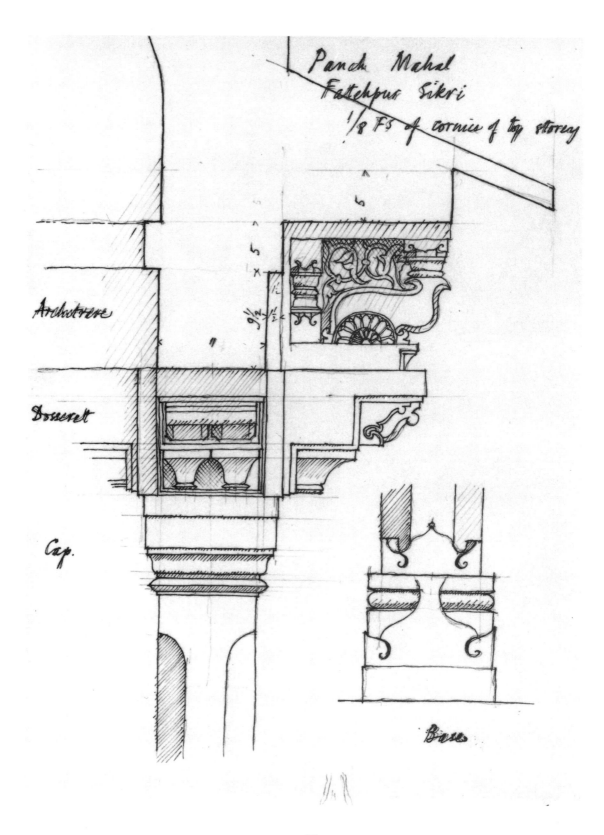

Panch Mahal
Fatehpur Sikri
1/8 FS of cornice of top storey

Architrave

Dosseret

Cap.

Base

68

Panch Mahal
½" scale

Entablature in
4th order at Panch Mahal
Fatehpur Sikri

28 Sept. 93

½" scale section of Cornice
in the Diwan-i-Amm.
Fatehpur Sikri
28 Sept 1993

Birbal's House, Fatehpur Sikri
Scale 1 pace = 1/4 inch

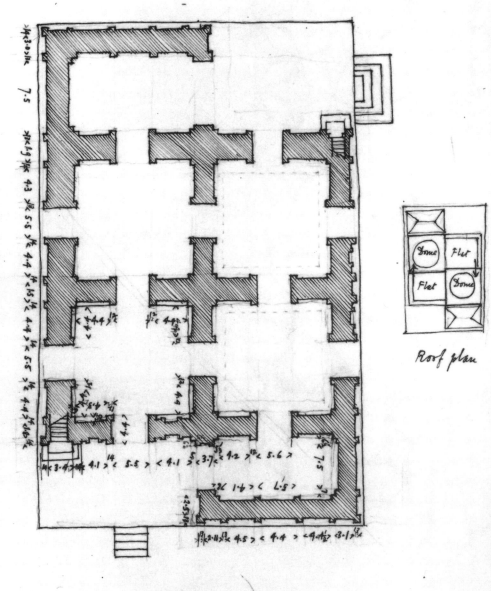

Roof plan

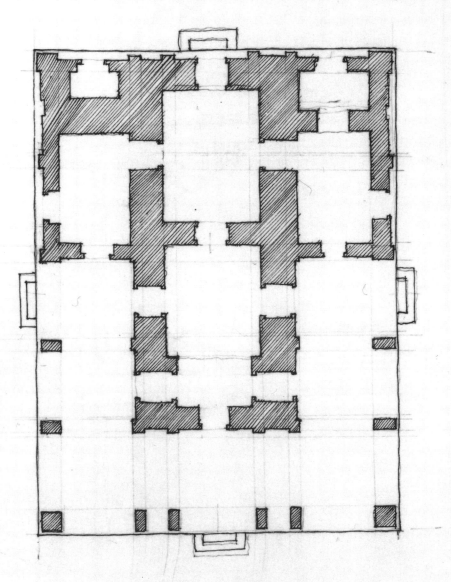

Miriam's House
Fatehpur Sikri

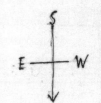

S
E — W

73

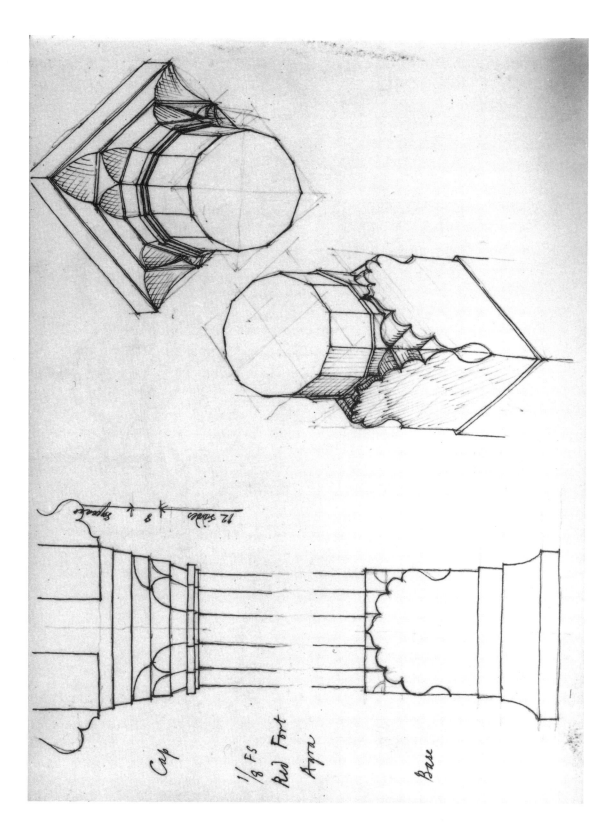

Cap

1/8 FS
Red Fort
Agra

Base

12 Stubos | 8 | Engrave

74

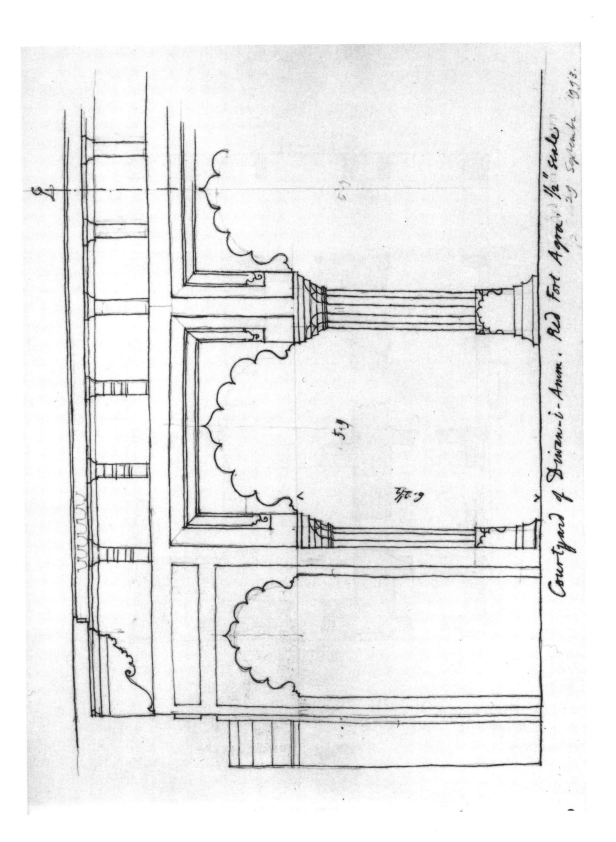

Courtyard of Diwan-i-Amm. Red Fort Agra. ½" scale
29 September 1913.

Niche in the Northern Palace of the Haramsara.
(Birbal's House) Fatehpur Sikri

1/8 F.S.

33

76

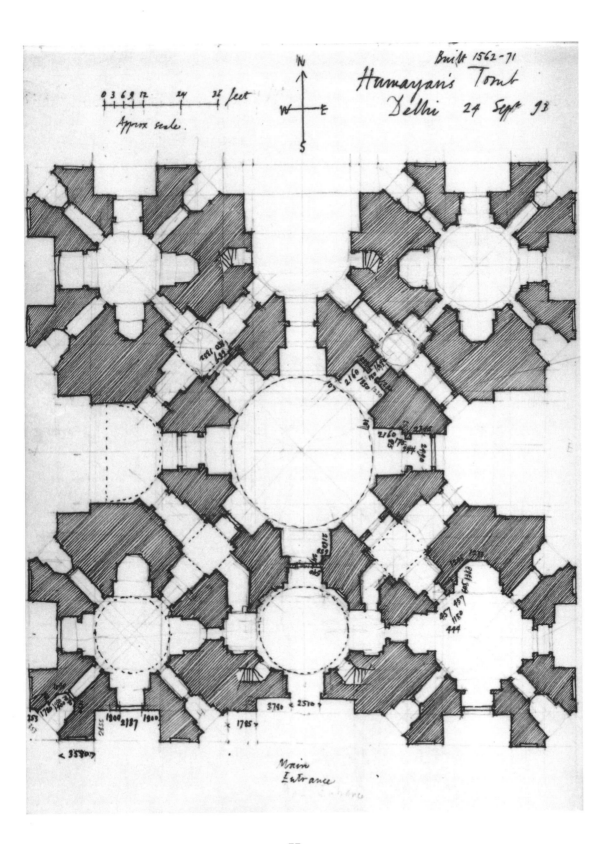

Built 1562-71
Humayan's Tomb
Delhi 24 Sept 93

0 3 6 9 12   24   3? feet
Approx scale.

N
W · E
S

Main
Entrance

77

Bulmer brick kiln

I went to see Mr L. A. Minter* on October 21st 1972 at his house at Bulmer, Sudbury, Suffolk to ask him how he made his domed brick kiln, which he built in 1936. I also measured it.

The construction is very simple. Having built a circular wall finishing 2' 7½" thick at the top, 6' 4" high and 17' 0" in diameter, he formed a circular skewback of two courses of plinth bricks as shown. He then laid the first ring of the dome using wet clay or pug for mortar. The virtues of pug are twofold: firstly because mortar would not stand the intense heat of the kiln and secondly because it is so sticky that the brick adheres to the skewback so tenaciously that it does not slip down before the bricklayer has laid a course of bricks right round the circumference & finished up where he started; by which time the first ring cannot slip down because it has become a circular wedge or voussoir. The process can now be repeated on the next course & so on until the dome is complete. As the rings become nearer the vertical there is a greater tendency for the bricks to slip down before the ring is complete but to counteract this the circumference is reduced so that it takes proportionately less time to complete the ring. He said that you can infact stick a brick with pug to a vertical surface for at least half an hour. As the dome settles soon after construction it tightens all the joints and therefore makes a more compact & homogenous dome.

The great virtue of this method of construction is that it needs no formwork or centering at all. It avoids a very costly & wasteful part of the work and provides probably the cheapest and most durable method of spanning an opening of these sort of dimensions.

Other information about this kiln.

It burns 12,500 – 14,000 bricks at a time for which it needs six tons of coal. It is fired by seven separate fires or bags shown on the sketch. Maximum temperature 12,000° centigrade. The fire goes up to the top of the dome & is then drawn down through the stack and away under the floor through radiating honeycombed sleeper walls & out at the side to the chimney.

The dome is restrained by two steel bands which are only necessary because of the thrust excerted as the dome rises and falls during each firing.

The kiln has been used continuously since it was built. The dome has never needed repair.

* Died two years later.

Bulmer brick kiln

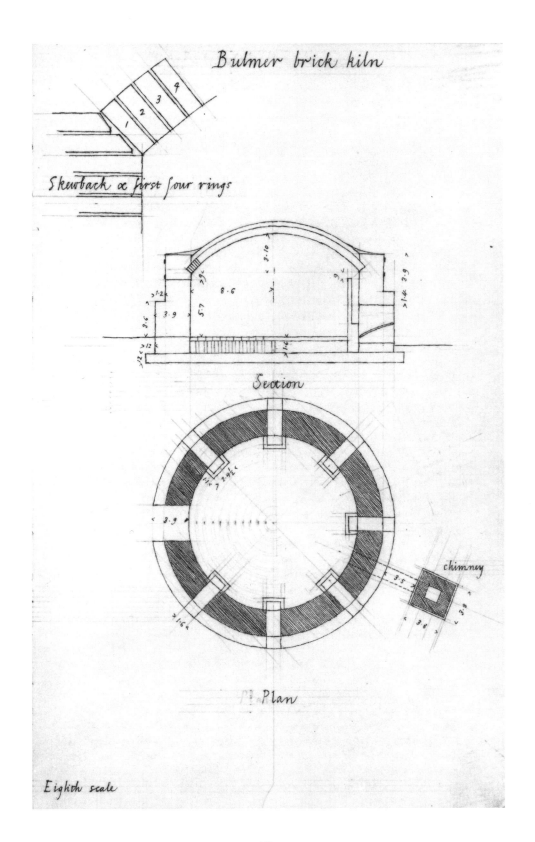

Skewback & first four rings

Section

Plan

Eighth scale

chimney

Eighth full-size detail of
main external cornice. Pantheon